How to be a
WELL BEING

How to be a WELL BEING

Unofficial Rules to LIVE Every Day

Dr Andy Cope, Jim 'Pouli' Pouliopoulos,
and Sanjeev 'Sanj' Sandhu
Illustrations by Amy Bradley

CAPSTONE
A Wiley Brand

This edition first published 2020

© 2020 Andy Cope, Jim Pouliopoulos, Sanjeev Sandhu and Amy Bradley

Registered office
John Wiley & Sons Ltd, The Atrium, Southern Gate, Chichester, West Sussex, PO19 8SQ, United Kingdom

For details of our global editorial offices, for customer services and for information about how to apply for permission to reuse the copyright material in this book please see our website at www.wiley.com.

A catalogue record for this book is available from the Library of Congress.

A catalogue record for this book is available from the British Library.

ISBN 978-0-857-08867-3 (paperback) ISBN 978-0-857-08870-3 (ePDF)
ISBN 978-0-857-08869-7 (ePub)

Cover design and illustration: Amy Bradley

Set in 10/14pt FrutigerLTStd by SPi Global, Chennai, India

Printed in Great Britain by Bell & Bain Ltd, Glasgow

10 9 8 7 6 5 4 3 2 1

For life and death are one, even as the river and the sea are one.

For what is it to die but to stand naked in the wind and to melt into the sun?

And what is to cease breathing, but to free the breath from its restless tides . . .

Only when you drink from the river of silence shall you indeed sing.

And when you have reached the mountain top, then you shall begin to climb.

And when the earth shall claim your limbs, then shall you truly dance.

From The Prophet *by Kahlil Gibran*

WELL BEING RULES

Three Authors, One Voice

An Englishman, a Greek/American, and a Welsh/Indian walked into a bar ...

Growing up, **Jim 'Pouli' Pouliopoulos** wanted to be a science fiction writer but he listened to his dad's advice and became an engineer because, 'You'll always have a good job, son.'

Thanks Dad!

Two engineering degrees, an MBA, and 20 years later Pouli realized he didn't want a 'good job' he wanted a fulfilling one, so he declared himself a 'recovering engineer' and he hasn't touched a drop of engineering since.

Instead, Pouli has found true happiness and success as a senior lecturer at Bentley University, which he combines with delivering 'The Art of Being Brilliant' in America. We figure Tony Robbins has had a good run but there's a new guy in town. Smaller and with better eyebrows, Pouli's expertise extends to all things 'wellbeing' so if you have a conference that needs pepping up with humour and positivity, he's yer man.

And boy is he qualified! Pouli was born to tell stories, something that shines through in his three (yes 3) TED Talks.

Pouli lives in Westford, Massachusetts, with his wife, Katherine, and a bunch of dogs. He's most proud that his three adult children listened to his advice and chose paths where they found their career calling and purpose early in life.

You can find Pouli online at www.POULI.com and on Twitter at @jimpouli.

Sanjeev 'Sanj' Sandhu is a one-off. Born in South Wales to English parents with an Indian origin, he was always going to be different. He studied accounting at a leading British university, worked for a couple of the biggest consulting firms on the planet, and then decided to put happiness first.

He is now thriving, working with his heroes at Art of Brilliance, spreading positivity across the world, and embracing the journey of life. Sanj delivers keynotes and workshops on themes of positive psychology, resilience, and mindset and is able to connect with audiences from age 6 to 106.

Sanj is an adventurer. Over the next 10 years he's focused on bringing 'The Art of Being Brilliant' to India and the Middle East but he's keen for you to know that, quite frankly, he'll go any-where on the planet.

Sanj is 30 years younger than his white middle-aged co-authors, which gives him a different perspective as well as boundless enthusiasm, freshness, and innocence that shine through in the pages that follow. And speaking of those pages, this is Sanj's first book but get excited because he is hungry for more . . .

You can find Sanj at www.artofbrilliance.co.uk or follow him at @sanjeevssandhu.

In comparison with his co-authors, **Dr Andy Cope** has been around the publishing block. He started out as a children's author with his 'Spy Dog' series running to 20+ titles. Then came a crunching gear change. Andy discovered the science of positive psychology in 2001 and loved the subject so much that he began a lifelong affair with it.

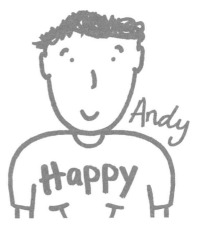

Twelve years later he gained a PhD in Wellbeing and after 20 years, Andy and Happiness are still going strong.

Their love child is a company called 'Art of Brilliance', which comprises a ramshackle bunch of wellbeing mavericks who think they can change the world. Andy and the team deliver keynotes and workshops globally and, hand on heart, believe the content to be the best in the world. The magic sauce lies in the fact that the messages from the science of human flourishing are all fairly obvious. Happiness is hidden in plain sight. Andy's job is to re-connect people with who they really are and get them to re-remember what brings joy into their life.

Just so you know, 'Art of Brilliance' is not-for-profit. Any money left over is ploughed into their Brilliant Schools projects. Getting young people immersed in positive psychology . . . that's the future, right there.

Andy is married to Louise and they have two grown-up children. The house feels empty and he misses the inane chatter of the young generation so is thinking of adopting Sanj.

You can check Andy out at www.artofbrilliance.co.uk or www.brilliant.school.

Twitter @beingbrilliant

Insta artofbrilliance

FB artofbrilliance

A Note from the Authors

This is a book for NOW because, gosh, how the world has changed! So rapidly and so dramatically.

At the time of writing we're in the grips of pandemic pandemonium which has triggered a financial and mental health meltdown so dramatic that we're probably going to have to redefine what 'normal' actually means.

Here's the truth – *the world is moving faster than human evolution*. We've been outpaced. And as the world changes, so do the damn rules. The game of life's difficult enough, but if you're playing by the old rules, you're doomed to finish amongst the also-rans.

To do more than survive – *to thrive and come alive* – you need to ditch the tired old wisdom.

For example: YOLO, you only live once. *Really?*

The truth is that you only *die* once. You get to *live* every single day. You just need to know how.

How to be a WELL BEING comprises twenty-two 'rules' that just are. Learn them, apply them and live by them because, best of all, they just work.

'Memento mori' – remember death. No more dicking around. No more wasting time. It's time to focus on what's most important and strive towards your true potential.

Welcome to your best life.

A Quick Word About Rule Breaking

you're a long time this

> *The modern way?*
> *He was found slumped at his computer, with his finger*
> *on the 'Escape' key.*

Before we introduce you to our rules, there's time to squeeze in three truths and a lie.

'Begin with the end in mind' is classic self-help fodder. So that's where we'll start. Excuse the bluntness of the next sentence but it's truth number 1:

> *You're a long time dead.*

Unfortunately, that sentence is not softened if you work the same information the other way. With eternity stretching into the past and present, the bare fact remains the same:

> *The act of 'being alive' is rather too brief.*

In all likelihood, if we average things out, you're going to get 4000 weeks of breathing. If you're under 10, that news lands well. There's a celebratory punch of the air as you suck on your ice lolly. The same stat for the under 25s is fair-to-middling, celebrated with a '#4000weeks' selfie posted to the various social media platforms. The over 50s tend to be less joyous. There's less fist pumping and more of a furrowed brow. *Really? I'm gonna live for 4000 weeks? Is that all? Is that even true?* (Before the day is out they will have Googled it, found it's true, and calculated how many weeks they have left.)

And there's genuine hilarity when you announce it to the over 85s. They just laugh in your face. They've used theirs up and are enjoying borrowed time. There's a twinkle. They'd do a heel click, *if they could!*

Our point *isn't* that you're going to die. We're guessing you've already worked that out for yourself. Our point is that life's a short and precious gift, so it makes sense to ensure your alive part is *properly alive*. You may as well do some stuff, shake your booty, and wave your arms around a bit before the music stops.

Which it will.

Because dirty little truth number 2 is that you can have a pulse but not be pulsating with life.

'Presenteeism' is a business word that's used to describe people who show up but go through the motions. They're logged on from 9.01 to 4.59, occupying a desk, sucking up oxygen, and drinking bad coffee, but they're not really there. Not fully.

Except 'presenteeism' isn't just about work. It can also apply to the rest of your 4000 weeks. Look around. There are a lot of people logged on, breathing, drinking coffee – but not many shaking their booty.

Our no-brainer of a question is therefore, if you're dead for almost all of eternity, and alive for such a brief flicker, isn't it worth making that pulse of yours race a bit? Isn't it worth putting a bit of effort into something a bit naughty, different, memorable, thrilling, or adventurous? Maybe even a little bit dangerous?

Or if that's too far, how about working at being more optimistic, hopeful, energetic, dynamic, and positive?

But there's a line to be drawn somewhere, right? We agree. You can overdo it. You'll have one or two in your circle who are smiling and ultra gung-ho, but not genuinely happy. Fake news is believable, but not fake happiness. Beware the grinogogs (an old English word for people who are so happy you want to punch them), with their faux smiles, annoying positivity, and fake silliness.

We're absolutely NOT into that. If you're annoying people with your zest for life, you're doing it wrong. Rather, we want you to take them with you on your journey. We want you to be infectious. In a wonderfully uplifting way.

Which begs the question, why are there not more of them? The infectious ones. The wonderfully uplifting human beings. The genuinely sparkling people who energize and inspire. Why is it that you can count them on the fingers of one hand?

The answer lies in human nature. We're social creatures. Pack animals. We're wired to fit into a team, tribe, clan, gang, family, community . . . we have an overwhelming desire to be part of something social. So, we look around at what everyone else is doing, and we copy, because when we look, sound, and behave like others, we belong. Humans crave a sense of belonging because it makes us feel safe.

Which is where it gets difficult. Safety is built into the human operating system. It's a basic need.

Our argument being that playing safe is all well and good. Fitting in is fine. But, on balance, standing out (for the right reasons) is a better place to position your 4000 weeks. And to stand out you have to dare to be different. And when you're different there's a chance of NOT fitting in!

Which leads us on to the third of our trilogy of truths:

> *If you're risking nothing at all, you're risking everything.*

When that pulse of yours pulsates for its very final time, it won't be death you're afraid of. You're more likely to be haunted by not having truly given life a damn good run for its money. There might be adventures not adventured, hikes not hiked, laughter not laughed, dances not danced, roller coasters not roller coasted, and swashbuckling unswashed. Or unbuckled? (We're not quite sure.)

And to dare to be different you sometimes have to be a bit of a rule breaker. Or at the very least a rule bender. Or if you're feeling particularly elfish, you can 're-imagineer' the rules. Which is what this book is about.

The problem with rules is just that. They've *always* been a problem!

In the beginning there was just one rule. God more or less told Adam he could do whatever he wanted, but 'Don't pick the bloody fruit. Okay?'

Adam probably looked around at the orchard, and then at Eve standing there in her fig leaf. 'What, anything?' he asked, looking his partner up and down.

'You got it', assured the big fella. 'You can have absolutely anything. But NOT my lovely red apples.' He glared at Adam just to be sure. 'Just one rule. No apples. *IS THAT CLEAR?*'

Adam nodded and rubbed his hands in glee (we're guessing, we weren't there).

And the rest, as they say, is history. Humanity's inability to resist apples was set in stone.

And 'stone' takes us on to Moses. With Adam messing up the first ever rule, Moses upped the ante and brought 10 of the damn things down from the mountain. On a tablet. Sure, there are some bangers in the original list and if we all lived by the #Moses10, the world would be a better place.

But here's the thing. Not only have tablets changed since Moses' day, but so has the world, and therefore so must the rules.

Just to be absolutely clear, we're not advocating that you become hell bent on breaking all of the rules all of the time. Thou shall not kill, steal, or ogle over next door's partner – these are decent rules that still have relevance in the modern world. There's also a host of more minor rules that you shouldn't mess with. For example, 'driving in the bus lane through the centre of Derby', even if it seems like a minor rule and even if you break it totally by accident, will still cost you £60.

To be fair to the modern world, the rules have moved on. If we take just one aspect of life – sport – the basics have stayed the same but the rules have been honed to make the game more exciting.

If you took the best soccer player from a hundred years ago and stuck him in today's English Premier League, he'd be bewildered. Not only new rules, but complex team formations, a plastic football, lightweight boots, super-sexy silky kit, a perfectly manicured pitch, and unprecedented levels of fitness. Your 1920s player would stand in his long shorts, clod-hopper boots, and flat cap, scratching his mutton chop sideburns in quizzical fashion as the game fizzed around him. If you told him there was a professional *women's* league he'd keel over in the mud.

That piece of kit between our ears has failed to keep pace with our environment. In evolutionary terms, you and I, *we are that player*. In the last decade the world has fizzed and buzzed. It's happened at warp speed. You're trying your hardest to keep up with life. In fact, the effort's exhausting you. Your brain's screaming Scotty's classic Star Trek line: *'I'm giving her all she's got captain'* and yet the Klingons of change continue to loom on your starboard bow. Warp speed isn't fast enough. Everything's accelerating, dazzlingly neon, and super-sexy.

'Everything', that is, *except us!*

Before we introduce our one and only lie, it's worth pausing to revise the three truths we've introduced in our opening salvo:

1. You're a long time dead.
2. You can have a pulse but not be pulsating with life. *And . . .*
3. If you're not risking anything, you're risking everything.

The big fat lie is that you need to work harder at keeping up. It's one of those unwritten rules that seems to have found its way into too many of us. We're lulled into comparing ourselves with our tribe, our fellow commuters, the airbrushed celebs . . . and working ourselves to the bone in an effort to stay relevant. Envy runs rampant in this day of social media and FOMO. If you want lower stress, less on your mind, and some of that weight removed from your shoulders, here's some BREAKING NEWS: doing the same, but harder, won't work. You'll just get *more* stress, *more* on your mind, and *more* weight on your shoulders.

It's time to rethink your thinking. If you're sick and tired of being sick and tired, and the *same old same old* isn't cutting it, instead of more of the same, how about trying *less of something completely different*.

Clear that muddle from between your ears, quieten the shouty inner voice, dare to leave some things unticked on your to-do list, stop trying to be perfect, and start to be amazing.

We're about to present 22 'rules of life'. Rules of *modern* life, to be precise. Re-imagined, re-engineered, re-thought, and re-remembered, our rules vary from the obvious and simple through to counter-intuitive and downright challenging. It is our hope that you take them in the manner in which they're intended. We're grappling with some big issues in a light-hearted way, but don't misinterpret our 'light touch' for light content.

Beware the clocks. They're watching you. They're not ticking their time, they're ticking *yours*. Every second counts.

Phasers set to stun.

Let's do it.

Rule #1

LIFE ISN'T FAIR (BUT THEN AGAIN, NOBODY EVER SAID IT WAS)

> Revenge in the modern world
> '…and Alexa, make sure they don't feel any pain.'

An open letter to our readers:

Dear highly valued book buyer,

First up, congratulations on such an excellent choice of book. We hope you enjoy every last page, even the ones you find challenging. Which is basically this page . . .

If you found a magic lamp and gave it a rub, these would be our wishes for you . . .

From time to time in the years to come, we hope you will be treated unfairly. Several times in fact. Frequently enough so that you will come to know the value of justice. We hope you also learn a bonus lesson from your unfair treatment – to move onwards and upwards with a smile on your face.

We hope that you will suffer betrayal because that will teach you the importance of loyalty. Sorry to say, but we also hope you will be lonely from time to time. Not big bouts of loneliness, they're plain horrible, just long enough that you learn never to take friends and family for granted.

We also wish you bad luck, again, from time to time, so that you will be conscious of the role of chance in life and understand that your success is not completely deserved and that the failure of others is not completely deserved either. And when you lose, which you will (frequently), we hope some of your opponents will gloat over their victory. Indeed, it helps if they actually mock you because during these times you will understand the importance of sportsmanship.

We hope you'll be ignored so you know the importance of listening to others, and we hope you will have just enough pain to learn compassion.

We wish you illness, both minor and major. An occasional toothache or bad back is perfect to remind you to appreciate the fact that, most of the time, your body does a marvellous job of getting you around town. Please don't take this next sentence the wrong way, but we also wish you something more substantial, an ailment that's even bigger than man flu. We wish you a recoverable health scare but something that truly knocks you for six. Once you've crawled yourself back to health, we are confident you will have a refreshed attitude to the simple act of being alive.

Mentally, we wish you an occasional bout of something that robs you of your mojo, temporarily of course, but mild depression or a bit of anxiety can have rejuvenating properties. Indeed, learning to cope with your thoughts is one of life's biggest challenges.

Career-wise, we hope you don't nail every job interview and that, on occasion, inferior colleagues get promoted ahead of your good self. There will be a lesson to learn, although we're not entirely sure what that one is. Temporary gnashing of teeth is okay, but contrary to popular belief, the best revenge isn't to let their tyres down, it's to truly shine at work and make your employer wonder how they could have erred in their choice.

And if the magic genie had two more wishes, we'd save the biggest till last.

Firstly, love. We sincerely hope that you fall headlong into it, hook, line, and sinker, and that the relationship ends. We hope it feels like your life has been torn apart, and that's good, because it has. And after weeks of sobbing, we hope you learn to move on, stronger, with lessons learned, and with an enhanced ability to find better, longer-lasting love. We really hope that your bad experience doesn't stop you loving in the future. Rather, it makes you better at loving. Our hope is that you realize that being miserable because of a former relationship just might mean that the other person was right about you.

Which brings us to bereavement. Once again, please take this next sentence in the manner in which it's intended; we hope that, on occasion, someone close to you passes away. Elderly great-grandparents might be the easiest to cope with, but closer than that perhaps. And that it's gut-wrenchingly painful. We hope that, in time, you heal and move on in the understanding that that's how the circle of life turns. And that one day it will be you that's gone and that gut-wrenching feeling will pass down to the next generation like it has since humans were invented.

The point is that whether we wish these things or not, they're 100% going to happen. Every single one of them. Indeed, some will happen several times.

Some may call such instances 'tragedies' or 'plot-twists'. We will simply call them 'life'.

Life isn't fair but then, if you stop and think about it, nobody ever said it was. Try starting from the position that life isn't ever going to be fair and you'll feel your angst washing away.

Sure, some people seem to have more of it to contend with, but adversity is a consequence of being alive. And whether you benefit from the adversities above will depend upon your ability to see the message in your misfortunes.

Oh, and one last thing, remember, life also has its ups. Don't forget to relish those.

Oodles of love,

Pouli, Sanj, and Dr Andy

xxx

Rule #2

YOUR
MATTER MATTERS

a giant tortoise

a humming bird

your fave pet

you

what do you all have in common?

> As soon as I saw 'To Whom It May Concern', I knew it had been misdirected.
>
> *Ashleigh Brilliant*

If you've got an unemployed 30-year-old adult child still living in your house, thumbing away at their games console while you go out to earn a living, fear not. A new large-data study suggests *laziness* might be a fruitful strategy for survival of individuals, species, and even communities of species.[1]

To save you reading the article (because by no means is it a page turner), we can sum it up thus: the researchers analysed the metabolic rates of 299 species over a 5-million-year period only to discover that species that have gone extinct tend to have higher metabolic rates than those that are still living.

Basically, metabolic rate (the amount of energy an organism needs to live their daily lives) seems to matter, with slooooow being more favourable.

The authors of the report postulate that *'maybe in the long term the best evolutionary strategy for animals is to be lassitudinous and sluggish . . . instead of "survival of the fittest," maybe a better metaphor for the history of life is "survival of the laziest" or at least "survival of the sluggish".'*

Which opens up a new line of enquiry that we'd like to explore by playing a game.

---

[1] The results have just been published in the *Proceedings of the Royal Society, Series B* by a research team based at the University of Kansas.

Line up a giant tortoise, a hummingbird, your favourite pet, and you. Good looks aside, what else do they have in common?

The answer is that they're all born with about a billion heartbeats to spare. It's why the hummingbird with all its frantic flapping and pulsing heart rate gets 3 years while the plodding, chilled-out tortoise can expect 150 or more.

It's an interesting thought that also leads to a BIG question: what are you going to do with your one billion heartbeats? Please excuse our rounding errors, but one billion heartbeats equates to an average lifespan of about 28,000 days. And, oh my goodness, would you believe it, we come full circle to those pesky 4000 weeks that we introduced earlier.

In the interests of setting you up for a bumper package of happy, uplifting, fulfilling, inspiring, go-getting, energized weeks, it's important that you understand you're *not* made of slugs, snails, and puppy dogs' tails. Nor are you made of sugar and spice and all things nice. You are made of trillions of cells that somehow meld into something you call 'you', and rule #2 boils down to this: you are made of matter. You are pure energy with a battery life of about 4000 weeks.

Just like the tortoise, hummingbird, and favourite pet, you will receive a body. It's the physical you and just like a supermarket bag, your body's for life. The other thing about your physical form is that it's a gift. You didn't choose it. It was given to you. Like it or lump it, there is no receipt so you can't take it back or swap it for a better one.

It therefore makes sense to learn to love and appreciate it. Yes, even the wobbly, knobbly, sticky-out, imperfect bits. And seeing as you're stuck with your body, you may as well take good care of it.

We've written this book because we care about you. You matter to us. But here's the thing. Rule #2 is that it really matters that your matter matters to *you*.

If we ask you about who your first love was, we're secretly hoping that you will say your own name. Not narcissistic 'self-love' as in 'I'm so marvellous. Much better than anyone else', but 'self-love' as in 'look after number 1'. Self-care is the least selfish thing you will ever do. It's a keystone habit which means that if you get rule #2 right – if your energy is fully charged – all the other rules become a whole lot easier to apply.

Why?

Because it's really hard to give what you haven't got. If you haven't got energy, confidence, happiness, and zest, it's very hard for other people to catch those qualities off you. And why on earth should anyone else love you if you can't be bothered to love yourself?

Hence the absolute bedrock of flourishing is that you must take care of your *physical* self.

If you don't service your car it will keep going and keep going and then splutter a bit. And then it'll splutter a bit more. Some lights will illuminate on the dashboard – lights you know shouldn't be there – but you keep going, juddering forward, ever more slowly until eventually the car stops.

Your body is the same.

If you have a sneaky peek at the people around you, you'll see a lot of spluttering. There are a lot of metaphorical lights flashing on people's wellbeing dashboards. They are juddering along fuelled on caffeine and sugar, their engine about to seize up. Scientists refer to this as entropy. Everything tends to wear down, break down, or get messier as time goes on.

Entropy has an opposite – negentropy (true, we promise), which is about putting energy back into the system. In human form negentropy shows up as rejuvenation – a reinvigorated version of you with a spring in your step and a smile on your face.

The three physical keys to being fully charged are eat, move, and sleep. We've reserved a special chapter for sleep, so here's a reminder of the basics of eating and moving – so basic that you already know them. But 'knowing' and 'doing', they're not the same thing. Once your matter *matters*, you might want to start taking moving and eating more seriously and actually do them properly.

Humans are hunter-gatherers. The world has moved on faster than we have, so nowadays we hunt and gather in the supermarket rather than on the savannah, but our bodies are built to move. I promise you, your body *wants* to be fit. If 'exercise' came in pill form, it would provide the biggest boost to wellbeing and mental health ever invented. The benefits of enhanced energy, mojo, and mental health would change entire communities.

Your body is crying out to be exercised. So exercise it! Treat it to a brisk 30-minute walk every day or maybe a few sit ups and press ups. Some yoga, Pilates, a fun run, half marathon, weekly swim, or game of badminton on a Wednesday night. The physical you might appreciate a couple of trips to the gym every week.

Commit, not just for a week, but for life. It's a tad more effort than taking a pill. And that is where it all comes crashing down. The dreaded 'ef' word.

Effort!

That is why your matter needs to matter to you. If you care about being the fully charged zestful version of yourself, the effort somehow seems less effortful.

Food-wise, eat good food 80% of the time. None of the authors are nutritionists, so we will simply remind you of what you already know; you cannot out-exercise a bad diet, so get the basics right.

The best way to 'diet' is not to starve yourself. It's to feed yourself fully with nutritious food – greens, fruits, vegetables, slow carbs. (The same principle goes for your mind. Don't starve yourself of good thoughts. Fill yourself up with high-quality nutritious thoughts instead. Positivity is like kale for your mind.)

Anything naturally orange, dark green, red, yellow, or purple is generally good. Beige is generally bad. Never eat anything that has to be passed to you through your car window or delivered to your door by a man on a scooter. Oh, and that supermarket 'meal deal' might not be quite the nutritious bargain you imagined.

Get off the sugary drinks and onto that stuff that drops from the sky. Plenty of it. Doctor's orders.

There are no guarantees, but the smart readers will figure that if they look after themselves, they're likely to get more than a billion heartbeats. But the message might be even bigger than that.

Last week Dr Andy went to his grandad's funeral. It was a very sad occasion and Andy had a chance to reflect on what a 'stellar life' actually was. His grandad had had an okay one. At 84 he'd eked out a few more than his allotted 4000 weeks. He was a decent bloke who'd worked hard as a bus driver.

Andy decided two things:

First that he wanted to die peacefully in his sleep, like his grandpa did, not screaming and yelling like his passengers.

Second that he wasn't sure exactly how many heartbeats he had left, but he was going to treasure every single one from now on.

Bottom line? There's no escaping the ticking clock. Nobody gets out alive, not even the giant tortoise. So first base is to take care of yourself. Treat yourself well.

Rule #3

CELEBRATE! YOU'RE A LOTTERY WINNER

> *Coming, ready or not!*
> A great way to start a game of hide and seek but a terrible way to end sex.

It's easy to snuggle underneath the duvet of excuses. Life's not fair, right? There really is too much work pressure, your boss really is an idiot, it's impossible to ever get to the bottom of your emails, your department is about to be restructured (again!), your commute is genuinely too long, the alarm does ring too loudly (and too early), the weekends are short, it drizzles, you cannot get a doctor's appointment, the rush hour is anything but a rush, your salary isn't quite enough, there are no good movies on Netflix, trains run late, the current crop of politicians are the worst in living memory . . .

It's all true!

But it pays to give yourself a break. It's a massive advantage if you begin from the other end of the telescope. Let's roll back the years to when your mum and dad met. At some point they will have started dating, kissing, and fumbling awkwardly. I don't want to gross you out but in order for you to exist, your mum and dad must have had sex. Hopefully, it was just a one-off, and you can now get the image out of your head. The gross bit is what your dad did – he exploded about 500 million sperm into your mum. Sorry about that image, but it's both important and true.

That ejaculation was, in actual fact, your first outing. You swam for dear life and, out of *500 million*, you were the tadpole that got to the egg first.

You need to factor in the chances of your grandparents meeting and producing each of your parents was the same 1 in 500 million chance. And the whole mating game can be traced back through your lineage to whomever started the whole shebang.

It's sobering to realize that you are the arrowhead of human evolution. You are the result of a million generations of humans who managed to survive long enough to have sex. If that chain had been broken *just once*, you wouldn't exist. You are the best that evolution can currently do.

Yes, YOU!

Think of all the love, passion, effort, births, near deaths, narrow escapes from wolves, fevers, plagues, wars, and associated scrapes that all your ancestors have experienced – *ever* – and they went through all that, so that you could exist.

And in each pregnancy, *you* were the 1 in 500 million sperm that swam the fastest. *You* were the sperm that wanted life the most as you wriggled down your dad's urethra, barging the others out of the way.

You were focused. *You* got to the egg. *You* got life. The other 499,999,999 didn't.

So now you've got it, what next?

Keep doing it! Get in! You are *that* sperm! You are already amazingly successful, the gold medallist sperm front crawler (possibly more of a wriggler?)

Doesn't it seem rather lame to grumble about your lot? Does it really matter that your train is late or that the traffic is at a standstill? Is it worth lamenting a 6am alarm clock that heralds the start of a brand new day? A day of being alive. Are you going to report back to all the other 499,999,999 sperm that *it's drizzling outside so you were right not to bother'*.

Congratulations. You are the arrowhead of humanity. You were lucky to be born, which means you were born lucky.

Rejoice that, against all the odds, you're here at all. You have won the lottery of life.

Anything else is just a bonus.

Rule #4

REGRETS, YOU'LL HAVE A FEW

> **Thought for the Day:**
>
> *It's bad enough to lose other people – but when you lose yourself, then where are you?*

There's a well-worn saying about regrets and getting old. It goes something like 'elderly folk don't regret the things they have done, they regret the things they *haven't* done'. As with all these adages, it's well-meaning.

But flawed.

That parachute jump. The one where your parachute *didn't* open. Half-way down, you'll be regretting that, for sure.

But, hey, we get the 'live life fully' sentiment, so here's a real-life example.

This section is pure Pouli . . .

Jim Pouliopoulos, one of your trio of authors – the clue's in the name. I was born and raised in a tough, blue-collar city outside Boston, an all-American boy whose family hails from a small village in the Greek countryside. Sadly, my grandparents, Dimitrios and Despina, are long gone. Dimitrios was a bit of a character, very entrepreneurial. As a young man, he saved enough money to create the first mechanized wheat mill in the village where he lived.

And I think his creative genes must have passed down to my dad's older brother, Uncle Lazarus. He had what would nowadays be called a 'portfolio career'. Uncle Lazarus worked in the mill but was also a merchant. He would take his donkey and travel across the countryside, buying interesting things and bringing them back to the village. He opened up a general store in the centre of town which became the focal point of the village, a place for the community to gather, sit, and chew the fat.

As a young man, Uncle Lazarus had a great ear for music. He begged his father to let him leave the mill for a month and go take music lessons. My grandfather refused and refused and refused until eventually relenting, on the understanding that young Lazarus could have a month off – *unpaid* – and that if he wanted music lessons, he'd have to fund them himself. 'Tough love' in today's parlance.

Legend has it that Uncle Lazarus loaded up a donkey, headed out of town, and paid for his music lessons with bags of flour. After just one month he became quite a good violinist. He would put together bands of gypsies and they would travel from village to village playing music at local weddings. He once told me that he made more money as a musician than he ever did as a merchant, shopkeeper, or miller!

And it was Uncle Lazarus whom my brother and I went to visit in the summer of 1989. It was a magical six-day trip in which I learned so much, even though, on reflection, not a lot actually happened! We spent most of our time in my uncle's little general store. I would get there in the morning and we'd eat a little bit of breakfast. We'd sit and talk. Uncle Lazarus would regale us with tales of the old days and I'd come right back at him with the new days. 'Ancient Greece is all well and good Uncle Laz, but you should check out New England! It's buzzing!'

We developed a sort of routine over those six days. Each day, I could start to smell the shish kebab cooking and he would bring out some feta cheese and bread. And we'd sit and eat and talk some more. There was laughter. I remember a lot of laughter!

Around noon time, my uncle would disappear for a moment into the back room and re-emerge with a bottle of clear liquid. You see, in addition to being a miller, a musician, and a merchant, my uncle was also a moonshiner. Uncle Lazarus conjured a less-than-wonderful version of an alcoholic spirit called raki, which is kind of like ouzo but more potent and less palatable. It's one of those drinks that you can't down without pulling a face.

A couple of contorted faces later and the laughter had turned to violin playing and dancing. And, hey, I can't even dance!

So that was our week. It flashed by in its simplicity and joy. We said our goodbyes and as we hugged I noticed tears on my uncle's cheeks. He told me, 'I'm crying tears of joy because you're the first Pouliopoulos I've met that I could actually drink raki with. Your dad was kind of a lightweight.'

I felt sadness at having to leave the village but, hey, I had a flight to catch. I promised my uncle that I would come back to drink more raki and share a few more stories. It was a promise I meant to keep.

But here's the thing. I would love to tell you the story about the time I went back and Uncle Lazarus taught me how to make raki. I would love to tell you the story about the time when we looked inside his violin and noticed that there was an inscription that said *Antonio Stradivarius* and we wondered if it was for real. I would love to have asked Uncle Lazarus what was the best thing he ever bought on his travels, or the best wedding he ever played at, or what he thought might be the secret to happiness.

But I can't tell you any of those things because a few years ago my dad called me one day to tell me, 'Your uncle is gone. Uncle Lazarus passed away.'

When anyone passes away in the family, there's a sense of mourning and loss. For me, in that moment, the emotion that struck me was not so much the sadness of loss. Bubbling inside was a combination of shame and anger which I think might be best summed up as regret.

How could 20 years have gone by so quickly? Why had I promised that I would visit him – *and meant it* – but not done so? Sure, I spoke on the phone with my uncle a handful of times during those two decades, but my mastery of the Greek language is fair-to-middling and he didn't speak English at all, so it was never the same as sitting face-to-face. In the village. In the sunshine. Pulling raki faces.

It's only on reflection that I am able to sit back and ask myself how two decades could flash by with me never managing to follow through on a promise that seemed so important at the time. As John Whittier said, more eloquently than I ever could: '*Of all sad words of tongue or pen, the saddest are these: "It might have been!"*' For me, there are three lessons. The first is that 'alarms' go off in your life and you hit the snooze button. In my case, my wife, my children, and my parents always asked me, 'When are you going to go back and see Uncle Lazarus? You should go back before it's too late.'

My snooze button responses seemed genuine: 'I'll get back there when I'm not so busy' or 'I'll get back to see Uncle Lazarus when the time is "right".'

Eventually the snooze button stops working. You've overslept. You've missed out. Regrets, you'll have a few, but if you're open to learning from them, you won't have too many.

The second learning point is about Uncle Lazarus himself. *What a guy!* My uncle was 95 years old when he slipped away peacefully after a lifetime of adventures as a miller, a merchant, a musician, and a moonshiner. There's an old saying, 'don't die with your song still inside of you' and I like to think that would have been his motto. Uncle Lazarus didn't owe the world anything. He gave it all, music and everything.

Which naturally leads me to my third learning point: life is about the stories you *can* tell and when Uncle Lazarus passed away, I realized that regrets are the echoes of stories you *cannot* tell. I want to live my life so that when my 4000 weeks are done and dusted, the preacher won't have to tell lies at my funeral. In fact, I want there to be so many stories – and the stories to be so epic – that the preacher doesn't know which ones to leave out!

Cheers Uncle Lazarus. *Stin ygeiá sas!*

Life is about the stories. What will your stories be?

Rule #5

IT PAYS TO KNOW THE TRUTH ABOUT MONEY AND HAPPINESS

is happiness at the end of the rainbow?

money

> Willy Wonka: *'Don't forget what happened to the man who suddenly got everything he wanted.'*
> Charlie Bucket: *'What happened?'*
> Willy Wonka: *'He lived happily ever after.'*
> – *Charlie and the Chocolate Factory*

Welcome to one of the wordiest rules in the book. Money and happiness? Hang in there, it's complicated, but important.

Have you thought recently how you don't need anything? That feeling of abundance. That thought that you already have absolutely everything you need to be happy.

No, me neither.

In fact, I need a LOT of things.

First base, I *need* to be alive, and for that I *need* my health. I guess that requires a combo of decent food, clean water, physical activity, and a good health service for when things stop working.

I *need* family and friends. I *need* the people I love to love me back. And, my neediness means I *need* them to tell me they love me.

I also *need* my children to be healthy and to find their way in the world. I *need* them to be happy! The exclamation mark tells you that's a very big *need*. (Of mine. Which is weird to articulate because it suggests I *need* other people to feel a certain way so I can feel happy.)

I *need* money. In fact, I never have quite enough of that so I always *need* a bit more than I've currently got. And to earn money, I *need* a job, preferably one I like.

I *need* clothes and my material possessions. I also *need* my house. Maybe a slightly bigger one? With a bigger garden perhaps?

I *need* holidays, and two a year doesn't cut the ice. I *need* some shorter holidays to plug the gaps between my big holidays. City breaks, weekends away, that kind of thing.

I *need* to feel safe and secure. I *need* to feel good. And a nice environment helps that, so I *need* clean oceans, less plastic, and less litter. I *need* a beer on a Friday. Sometimes I *need* more than one. I *need* coffee – *lots of coffee* – otherwise I get tetchy. Coffee every day, not just on a Friday.

I *need* my mental health to be, well, *healthy*. So, sharpness of mind is important, along with memories. *Good* memories! And for good memories, I *need* to have had happy experiences to remember. And if I travel the timeline the other way, I *need* things to look forward to, placeholders in the future that are earmarked for some guaranteed happiness.

I even *need* the weather to be a bit warmer and less rainy than it is now.

I always *need* a bit more energy and confidence. I also *need* to feel a little bit more creative because it makes writing easier. I *need* happiness too. And I *need* all of these things in my nearest and dearest.

So, gosh, I'm so needy. But I'm guessing you are too?

And all of the above is true because you and I are real people with emotional and physical needs and desires that must be satisfied for us to be OK.

My thinking runs thus: *once I have those things, I will be content*.

And if that's true, it explains why I'm working so damn hard to satisfy my neediness.

But what if it's not true? Or, perversely, what if the exact opposite is true. Rather than *'once you have enough, you'll be content'* it's actually the other way around?

Once you're content, you have enough.

An even bigger 'what if?' lies in the notion of us being infected with psychological toxins. In the same way that junk food is distorting our bodies, what if junk values are distorting our minds?

What if materialism is McDonalds for the soul?

In the interests of remaining open-minded, I might be totally wrong. Materialism might be the best thing ever. Being persuaded to part with your hard-earned cash in exchange for an item that brings you a spike of happiness – that's how most people operate. Indeed, it's what entire economies are based on.

It's always useful to work things the opposite way. Think through some anti-materialistic logic. Imagine if you watched an ad and it told you the truth, which is: *Great news! You're perfectly fine as you are. You look okay. You smell reasonable. You haven't got dandruff. You're likeable enough. Most people have no beef with you. Your car is absolutely fine. Your carpets are clean. Your phone does what you want it to, plus it actually does a whole load of stuff you don't even know about. Your finances are passable. Your house is lovely. You've got enough shoes. You don't need any more stuff. Enjoy your life mate.*

It'd leave you with no desire to go to a retail park, lunge at your laptop to spend, or feed your face in a chain restaurant. Whoever wrote that advertisement would be sacked.

And if everybody learned the truth – *you don't need any more stuff* – the economy would come crashing down.

So, we're sold the opposite story. If we can be persuaded that the solution to our emptiness is to accumulate more stuff, the economic wheels keep turning and the advertising teams keep thinking of new ways to make us needy. And that's how your 4000-week game plays out.

Plus, you've been on the materialist treadmill for so long it's actually quite difficult to step out of the game. In fact, for most people, it's hard to recall ever NOT being in pursuit of more.

If you ask a bunch of school kids, *'Who wants to be a millionaire?'* 100% of hands will go up, ramrod straight. There's an outbreak of beaming faces and excited chatter, *'Oh, yes please!'*

Whereas if you ask the same crowd, *'Who wants to be happy?'* you'll still get a lot of hands, but less ramrod. In the flush of youth, there's a bit of ambivalence about happiness, but total certainty about filthy lucre.

As we age, we wise up. A bit. But to be properly money-savvy, it pays to know the truth about income and happiness. It's a confusing relationship, so prepare yourself for some brow-furrowing.

The so-called 'Career Happiness Index'[1] produces a league table of happy occupations. Florists and gardeners are top (87% of them are happy), with hairdressers and plumbers close behind. May we point out the bleeding obvious – none are particularly high-earning jobs. Just to prove that the universe works in wondrous ways, bankers came bottom with only 44% of them experiencing happiness.

Just to be clear, if you plot income and happiness on a graph, at no point does having more money make you less happy. So, while it's *technically* true that money can't buy happiness, it can buy choice, comfort, and airline tickets to somewhere with palm trees. Or, to paraphrase rock god David Lee Roth, trinkets, watches, and luxuries aren't everything but if you DO have money you can at least buy a big yacht to sail right up close to them.

If you ask people to rate their happiness on a 1–10 scale, the world average hovers around 5. But the Happy Planet Index shows huge geographical variations. At the time of writing, this oft-quoted international league table of happiness has Finland at the top (their citizens averaging 7.8), closely followed by Denmark, Norway, Iceland, the Netherlands, Switzerland, and Sweden. It's interesting to note that of the mighty G7 – whom the IMF describe as the richest and most developed nations in the world – only Canada makes it into the Happy Planet Top 10 (currently in ninth spot, scoring an admirable 7.3).[2]

---

[1] http://www.cityandguilds.com/news/November-2012/careers-happiness-index-2012#.WPSOcojytnl.
[2] The Happy Planet Index confuses the happiness issue slightly by using 'sustainability' as one of the weightings. But it remains one of the world's most respected and quotable happiness measures.

What do the Top 10 nations have in common? They're all well-developed countries with modern economies, decent infrastructure, good healthcare/education, and are currently peaceful. Oh, and they all happen to have cold winters.

If we cherry-pick a few notables from the chasing pack; the UK is 15th, the USA 19th, the super-powers of Russia and China are 68th and 93rd, respectively, with India coming in at a lamentable 140th (averaging 4.0, 'must try harder!')

The best-performing non-first-world nation is Costa Rica, punching well above their weight at number 12. Incidentally, and this may or may not be related to the Ticos' lofty league table position – Costa Rica is the only nation on the planet that *doesn't* have an army.

Hot countries occupy the bottom of the league table. In last place (156th) is South Sudan (scoring a miserable 2.9), propping up the Central African Republic, Afghanistan, and Tanzania. Geographically, most of the bottom 20 do not appear in the travel brochures, being either sub-Saharan, war torn, or both.

So, other than *'don't book your summer holidays in South Sudan'*, what does this tell us?

Here's the messy bit. As the league table shows, rich nations are generally happier so, yes, your general standard of living will affect your happiness. You've got a better chance of being happier if you're Finnish than Sudanese. But so will your *relative* standing. We don't want to belittle whatever's going on in sub-Saharan Africa, but the so-called Easterlin Effect suggests that it's very difficult to raise what we'll call 'gross domestic happiness' because, as the economy grows and everyone earns more money, our relative pecking order remains the same so we don't feel any happier.

> *'A rising tide lifts all boats.'*
>
> *– Popularized in a John F. Kennedy speech in 1963*

That partly explains why the UK and USA's happiness has flatlined since the 1940s. In the UK, disposable income has risen ninefold, which means you have nine times more spending power than your great-grandparents, and yet, as a nation, we are not a single percentage point happier. The phenomenon of *everyone's* income rising ninefold means that we don't feel any different because our position in the pecking order is the same.

Next up, to muddy the waters even further, the link between money and happiness weakens as income rises. In essence, people on very low incomes will experience increases in happiness, but only up to a certain point. The exact point is debatable, but roughly equates to a household income of about £50k.[3] In simple language, the difference in happiness between earning £15,000 and £30,000 is substantial, whereas the difference between £1,000,015,000 and £1,000,030,000 is negligible and £1,000,000,015,000 and £1,000,000,030,000 is a rounding error.

Here's an activity to set up our next point.

---

[3]https://www.forbes.com/sites/learnvest/2012/04/24/the-salary-that-will-make-you-happy-hint-its-less-than-75000/#7822d2683247.

Take 5 minutes off, grab a pen and paper, and list the top 10 happiest *moments* of your life. In fact, we'll create some space for you below. Go on, do it, right now.

Happiest *moments* of my life (so far):

1. _____
2. _____
3. _____
4. _____
5. _____
6. _____
7. _____
8. _____
9. _____
10. _____

We hazard that there are no products on your list. It will consist entirely of experiences – *with people you love* – and probably with no Wi-Fi.

Doing away with league tables and clever sciency stuff, here's how to squeeze maximum happiness value from your limited funds – spend less on things and more on *experiences*. So instead of buying more stuff, *do* more stuff. Or, if you really have an itchy spending finger, spend your hard-earned cash on a product that allows you to have an experience; a mountain bike, a concert ticket, running shoes, gym kit, a book, a tent, a dog, a snow-board, a Glastonbury ticket, or a picnic hamper.

Further, you tend to get more happiness from lots of smaller experiences rather than one big splurge. So, for example, several short breaks will buy you more happiness than one 3-week all-inclusive blowout.

Digging deep, if we piece some of the learning together, it would seem that to be truly happy we have to switch off our factory setting of 'social comparison'. That's more difficult than it appears, because of the viral nature of advertising. Research shows that people who desire more money or material wealth tend to be unhappier, so a celebrity-obsessed world of retail therapy is setting itself up to fail. The nuanced point is this. Money will make you happy. Buying stuff creates a spike of pleasure. But the *relentless pursuit of more stuff* will make you unhappy. The trick is to know when you've got enough. Perhaps Seneca was right when he said, *'It is not the man who has too little but the man who craves more that is poor.'*

Learning to be happy with what we've got, rather than falling for the marketing con of lusting after whatever they're pushing . . . there's a certain smugness in quitting the chase. It requires you to turn down your 'comparison-ometer' and, in time, you begin to get pleasure from that too. It's quite calming to know you don't have to match up to everyone else's possessions.

It's a messy chapter so here's a summary of the learning:

1. You're fortunate if you're born into a wealthy, developed, cold-wintered country.
2. Money doesn't guarantee happiness, but it sure helps smooth the way.
3. In terms of possessions, less might indeed be more.
4. 'Stuff' will bring you instant but short-lived happiness. It can also bring debt. To squeeze more value from your happiness pound, spend it on experiences.

5. Or, if you want to buy a 'thing', buy something that facilitates an experience.
6. Our primitive brain keeps digging us deeper into the moreish arms race. Waiting for everybody else to change is pointless. You'll die waiting. We dare you to be happy with what you've already got.
7. Social comparison is difficult to switch off. Use it to your advantage by comparing downwards if you want to feel lucky and upwards to feel driven.
8. Consider retraining as a plumber or florist.
9. Don't book your next holiday in South Sudan.

Rule #6

SAY 'THANK YOU' (IT REALLY IS THAT SIMPLE!)

> *'Feeling gratitude and not expressing it is like wrapping a present and not giving it.'*
> William Arthur Ward

Weirdly, the most amazing facet of your 4000 weeks – *the actual notion of being alive* – is easy to take for granted. We've got so much clutter and so many thoughts vying for our attention that the sublime awesomeness of simply *being alive* somehow slips our minds.

In fact, it's easy for our thoughts to migrate the other way and for your 4000 weeks to become a plodding and monotonous drudgery, existing from one holiday to the next. It takes no effort whatsoever for your head to be filled with self-doubt and needless worry.

But relax, it's not just you. Everyone you meet, and everyone you simply walk by, is experiencing this inner dialogue which veers to the negative and conjures up feelings of self-doubt.

It's actually quite comforting to know that even those people who seemingly have their shit together actually don't.

You can't turn the shouty inner voice off (it's built into your human operating system), but you can learn to turn it down whilst simultaneously turning the gratitude amplifier up to full whack.

But how can you learn to step aside and let the sunshine in?

You can start with a change in perspective and a pat on the back. Congratulations, you are a fully paid-up lifetime member of the most exclusive club in the history of humankind. You are a member of the most in-debt, medicated, obese adult population in the history of the human race.

Woo-hoo!

The world has always been a dangerous place. The terror used to come from scarcity – not enough food, clean water, warmth, or medicine. Today, the world is still dangerous, but the terror pendulum has swung from extreme lack to gratuitous excess. Nowadays, it's not appendicitis that finishes you, it's the addiction to your prescribed painkillers.

We're the first generation – *ever* – to be killed off by excess. We're dying of ailments caused by over-consumption of food, drink, and medication. Obesity, type 2 diabetes, heart attacks, alcoholism, stress, addictions: the modern world is killing us. Our ancestors indulged in impossible dreams of exactly the same conditions that we find ourselves in today . . . warmth, safety, food, drink, comfort . . . but mother nature has designed us to operate as perpetual dissatisfaction machines.

If you got into a DeLorean, powered the flux capacitor, and went back in time to collect your *great-great-great-great-great-great-great-great-great-great-great-great-great-great-great* grandma you'd have to be sure to set the dial to a point before her 45th birthday. Otherwise, when you turned up, she'd have been dead. Killed by the harshness of life. Either cut down in childbirth or brutally mown down by starvation, typhoid, appendicitis, or a particularly harsh winter.

Assuming you were able to catch her before her early demise, and you bundled her into your DeLorean, whizzing your dear great[16] gran into the 2020s, what would she have made of it?

The ubiquitous availability of food. Houses with central heating. Someone to help deliver your babies and operate on your appendix. A guaranteed harvest. Flushing toilets. *Inside* the house! Taps, with clean water. One of the taps even dispenses *hot* water! A bunch of guys turning up to take your rubbish away. Electricity. Wi-Fi. Foreign travel. Wardrobes overflowing with clothes, with a washing machine to clean them. And shoes! So many pairs of shoes! Your *great-great-great-great-great-great-great-great-great-great-great-great-great-great-great* gran has two pairs back at home: one pair of boots for working in the fields, and another for working in the house.

She would look at your abundant lifestyle and the shock might kill her! The old woman would have a tear in her eye. The life of comfort and safety, all she ever dreamed of, and it's right here.

You are living it. But are you loving it?

One of the first phrases we are taught as children is to say 'thank you'. It's good manners. But what if 'thank you' is more than just being polite? When we are saying 'thank you' we are being grateful. Gratitude, in its most simple form, is to be thankful for something or someone. While we are being thankful for something, it negates anger and fear.

When was the last time you felt grateful for all that you have?

Gratitude is the recurring theme of Dr Andy's happiness research, and of almost all the academic papers ever produced. It's also the golden thread of most religions. Gratitude is also blindingly obvious and oh so simple.

All three of your authors have learned to come at life from a bedrock of gratitude, but Sanj is a ninja. He lives and breathes it. And according to Sanj, there are various ways to exercise your gratitude muscles.

When I was 24 and just embarking on this journey of personal wellbeing, I decided to up my gratitude bar. I began expressing three things I was grateful for every single day as part of my personal 'happiness challenge'. Initially it felt a bit odd – a bit cringe and rogue if I'm honest – but after a few days of consciously taking time out of my day (first thing in the morning, before getting out of bed or in the shower 99% of the time) I realized that my mood was uplifted. For me it was even more invigorating than a morning workout. Everything seemed brighter, the world was full of colour, and life seemed a whole lot easier. It was bliss. At the time of writing these words I am on day 562 of expressing three gratitudes a day.

Remember, your brain is very good at picking out the negatives. Most people spend a massive amount of their life moaning about what they haven't got. Please don't be 'most people'. Learn to live from the opposite standpoint.

Write a list of 30 things that you're lucky to have but that you take for granted. It'll be an eclectic list of people, health, the things that your great-great- . . . great gran marvelled at, and more. Leave the list by your bed and when the alarm awakens you on the morrow, wipe the sleep from your eyes, get them fixed on your list, and skip your way to a flushing toilet, hot shower, and fluffy towel. It's no longer a rude awakening, it's a spiritual and joyous one.

Gratitude refocuses your attention. The grass isn't greener anywhere else. Its verdant lushness is right here, right now. Once I started to focus on celebrating what I have got, I questioned what on earth the old me had been chasing in the first place? Those stupid hours I was putting in at the office; what would that additional money be spent on? What would that next holiday give me? What would the next party provide (apart from being sleep deprived the next day)?

At a deeper level, my attitude of gratitude was an emotional check-in. It taught me to slow down, look around, and notice what's good. That fuelled the inner me and the outer me would follow suit.

If Sanj's passion hasn't gripped you, then this true story undoubtedly will. A few years ago, Dr Andy ran a workshop for a group of deaf women in Derbyshire. It was a Saturday morning freebie. Audience deafness presented me with some presentational challenges. The painful truth be told, I'd already done a 60-hour week and could have done without the hassle.

Three hours later, I drove home in floods of tears. Not through epic failure but through humility and a massive change of perspective. They were astonishing women, their challenges far greater than anything I've ever had to overcome. One young woman sat in the front row, beaming at me from start to finish. She had a T-shirt emblazoned with 'STAY POSITIVE', which I thought was pretty cool. We did a selfie at the end and she confided that she didn't mind being deaf; it was her brain tumour that was causing her more grief.

And I'd been grumbling about working on a Saturday morning?

Amen.

Rule #7

IT'S OKAY TO
NOT BE OKAY

This chapter
was very
nearly this:

A blank page

> **Challenge of the Day:**
>
> *You've got to ignore the craziness around you, in order to deal with the craziness within you.*

Admission time. This was actually going to be a blank page. Like totally pure white, not even a page number. The emptiest page a book has ever seen.

But then we thought, hang on, whoever's bought this book will expect to get their money's worth. Books need pages and words. So if we do a page with no words the readers will think we're ripping them off. They'll send nasty letters. *'Dear authors, we want our money back. How dare you leave an actual blank page? If you don't refund my book money immediately, I'll find out where you live and you can be sure I'll be posting some dog poo through your letter box.'*

And you'd have signed the letter 'Angry from Manchester', with absolutely no kisses.

And rightly so. A blank page with no explanation would have confused you. Hence, instead of a blank page, we decided to use the space to explain *why* it was going to be a page of nothingness.

You probably think that writing books is easy. That words just magically appear.

We promise you, they don't. The day starts with an empty page of nothingness, staring right back at you. The writer has to think of some words and then get them down on paper, in the right order, so they make sense. With punctuation and everything.

And when we're not feeling it, no words appear. Or, even worse, the sentences are rubbish and there are loots of spilling mistokes.

Basically, I was going to leave it blank because, that day, I couldn't think of anything to write. I was feeling a bit, you know, *meh*. Dreary. Not much energy or creativity. It left me feeling like I couldn't be bothered. I was being me, but in low-battery mode.

But here's the thing. For the record, I have studied happiness and human flourishing for the best part of two decades. My PhD involved me seeking out happy people and interviewing them, teasing out their wisdom and sharing it with the world. Their strategies are clear, simple, and understandable. Best of all, they're do-able, and I've embedded said habits into my life . . .

And yet, on occasion, I still have a bad few days. Empty pages in my 4000-week story.

I've had a special tee-shirt printed for just such days. It's got two words emblazoned on the front – 'YES' and 'NO', both in shouty bold – and it clears up 95% of my conversations. When people find out that I'm a 'Doctor of Happiness', the first thing they invariably do is laugh in my face (the sublime irony that my job title has immediately made them happy often passes them by) and when they've finished chuckling they ask, 'Happiness. Is that an actual thing you can be a doctor of?' and I point to the 'YES'.

They nod a while as it sinks in that I'm the total opposite of a normal doctor. I haven't beavered away for 6 years studying ailments and maladies, I've locked myself away for double that time, studying people who shine. I know very little about illness. I guess I'm an un-doctor.

And when they've processed the quirk of my job title their comeback is invariably, 'So does that mean you're always happy?' and, on a *meh* day, I can point emphatically to the shouty 'NO'.

To be clear, the appliance of science means I don't have to wear my shouty tee very often. My bad days are rarer than a blue moon, but despite me being a scholar of all things happy, those bad days do exist.

There's a technical term for it. It's called *'being human'*.

Hence, rather than a totally blank page, we've offered you this explanation. And I guess the point is that it's perfectly normal to have off days.

Just because you're struggling doesn't mean you're failing.

If your life is a book, it's okay to have an occasional blank page.

It's okay to *not* feel okay.

It's perfectly alright *not* to feel alright.

It's absolutely normal to feel *abnormal*.

It's fine to *not* be fine – have you got the point yet, or do I need to do one more?

It's perfectly reasonable to feel *unreasonable*.

Nobody feels amazing all the time. Life sometimes gets in the way. Even happy people get sad.

The trick is to not have too many 'okay', 'alright', 'abnormal', 'fine', or 'unreasonable' days.

But when you're having one (which you will), notice that you're having it and make a determined effort to bounce back the next day. Come back fully charged.

Too many blank pages make for a very dull book!

The rest of the book will tell you how to have an amazing life. Meantime, if any actual blank pages crop up, you now know why.

Thank you. Now, on to rule #8 . . .

Rule #8
SLEEP EASY

"Must have coffeeeeeee"

> **Thought for the Day:**
>
> *Biotics: are you pro or anti?*

A parable of modern medicine . . .

The first thing Dr Sandman did was prick my finger and take some blood. While that was being analysed she got to work prodding and poking me. I'd opened wide and said *'aaaaaaaaaaah'* as she shone a light on my raw throat and fuzzy tonsils. She'd nodded to herself and scribbled a few notes. She'd wrapped an armband around my arm and pumped hard – thrice – then left the room to collect my blood report as I rolled my sleeve down. I sat in silence wondering what *'150 over 90'* actually meant in plain simple English.

The doctor bristled back into the consultation room, piece of paper in hand. I was pleased there were no rubber gloves and no instruction to 'drop your trousers, lie on the couch, and turn onto your side'.

'What's the news doc?' I asked, attempting a weak smile. 'Am I gonna live, or is this sore throat the end of me?'

Doctor Sandman wasn't for smiling. She handed the prescription slip to me and instead of some unintelligible doctor-scrawl, there was one word written in all caps: 'SLEEP'.

'What's this mean?' I asked.

She looked at me gravely. 'It's a fairly simple concept. You need more sleep. A full eight hours a night. *Every* night. I'm worried about some things I noticed during your exam. The tonsils. The sore throat. Blood pressure on the high side. Cholesterol, same. That run-down feeling. I am prescribing sleep for you as a preventative measure.'

I chuckled, going along with the gag. 'Nice one doc. But everyone knows sleeping is cheating. Sleeping is for wimps. I've got a lot on. I just need some pills off you to perk me up. I'll sleep when I'm dead . . .'

The doctor cast me a withering look and interrupted. 'That's my point. It's my job to keep you from being dead for as long as possible.' 'And', she added, 'to ensure your alive time is truly alive. Sleeping isn't cheating, it's *treating*. And it's not for wimps, it's for *winners*. Quite frankly, if you don't change your current sleep regime, you'll be dead a lot earlier than you anticipated.'

'Oh . . .' I wasn't sure what else to say. The doc wasn't in jokey mood. 'But eight hours? That's like a third of an entire day.'

'It isn't *like* a third of an entire day. It *is* a third. Think of it as an investment in your other two-thirds. Sleep. That's all I prescribe these days. Well, that and exercise. Sleep is the most effective health supplement in the world and takes eight hours to digest. All doctors should prescribe it.'

'They should?'

'It'd save the health service. It's totally free. It's the ultimate wonder drug but despite its massive health benefits, most of my patients fail to take the prescription.'

'They do?' I asked, wondering how on earth I was going to conjure up a magical three extra hours a night.

'They put it off and decide they're going to catch up on their sleep on vacation or on the weekend. They're busy people. And in a busy life it's easy to edge sleep out so you can cram in more emails, Netflix, scrolling, nights out, office hours . . . but it doesn't work like that.'

'It doesn't?' I asked, astonished that she knew the exact details of my routine.

'Your lifestyle, your job, and society as a whole is stacked against you on this one. Answer me this, do you need coffee to kick-start your day? And by 'need' I mean *neeeeed*'. 'Must have coffee . . .' said the doctor, doing stiff Zombie arms.

I was relieved to see some mild humour showing up, at last. 'Well, yes, but . . .'

'No buts', butted the doctor. 'Get eight hours of sleep tonight, and every night this week. In fact, call me this time next week to report how you're getting on. Doctor's orders!'

'That's it? No pills for my throat?'

'No pills for your throat. Just this', she said, tapping the prescription. 'Your smartphone has a battery. It needs plugging in otherwise it stops working. You get a warning message, then a red bar, then nothingness. Blank screen. Am I right or am I right?'

She didn't wait for an answer. 'You're in the red zone.' There was an ominous pause. 'One away from a blank screen.'

I gulped at her bluntness as she pushed a pencil and notepad across the table. 'Here's some information. Make notes if you want to.'

She was off before I had time to pick up the pencil. 'Researchers have shown that we need eight hours of sleep to perform at our best day in, day out. Everyone knows that eight-hour rule but most dip way below. We average about six hours of sleep on a consistent basis and that has serious health and wellness implications. If you sleep less than six hours a night, you suffer from sleep deprivation which has been proven to impact your body and mind in a number of nasty ways. People who sleep less than six hours a night . . .'

She nodded at the pencil. I sat up and got ready to write . . .

'. . . have a 45% increased chance of developing coronary heart disease. Are *200%* more likely to have a heart attack or stroke and show symptoms of being pre-diabetic – even if they are not. If you don't get your full sleep allocation you may well have higher blood pressure. Also, less sleep leads to significant weight gain', she said, pausing just long enough to glance at my paunch. I shifted uncomfortably, sucking in as best I could. 'Sleep-deprived people crave carbohydrates, sweets, chips, and crisps.' I blushed a little as she glanced at the bag of salty pretzels peeping from my backpack. 'Sleep-deprived people eat 300 more calories per day on average. Those extra calories lead to an annual weight gain of 10 to 15 pounds.'

I scribbled as fast as I could, fuelled by embarrassment if I'm honest.

'In men, sleep deprivation results in lower testosterone and 29% fewer sperm and in women, it causes 20% loss in follicular-releasing hormones which are critical in the development of fertile eggs. Sleep loss makes you more susceptible to illness – flu, sore throats, that kind of thing – and I'm going to spare you the cancer stats.'

I looked up from my scribbling. 'Spare me?'

'Otherwise you'll be so scared you won't sleep', she smiled. 'There are also suicide and Alzheimer's implications', she said, almost offhand. 'Google them.'

As I was struggling with how to spell *alz-hei-mer*, she launched into some more big words. 'Your sleep patterns are driven by your circadian rhythm – everyone has one, and we're all a bit different. Humans have split the day into 24 equal chunks, but most circadian rhythms are longer than that and can run as long as 28 hours. That means some people have longer 'internal' days than others. Basically, there's a bundle of nerves called the suprachias-matic nucleus which sits in the middle of your brain. This bundle monitors the light sensed by your eyes. It can sense light hitting your eyes even when your eyelids are closed. When the bundle senses light, it tells your brain that day has begun. Your suprachi-asmatic nucleus synchronizes your circadian rhythm to start a new cycle and begin a brand new day.'

I was writing *'Super-cali-fragi . . .'* as she ploughed on.

'Here's the problem. The light emitted by all our smartphones, tablets, and laptops causes false triggers in this bundle of nerves. So, for example, if you try to fall asleep at night with the television on, your brain is sensing the light and telling your body that a new day is beginning. Meanwhile, your body has released melatonin into your blood stream as a sort of starting pistol for the sleep process to begin. Your biology gets confused.'

I nodded, unsure of the big words, but sold on the science.

'Everyone has a natural, preferred sleep pattern. Are you an owl or a lark? Night or morning person?'

'I'm probably a bit owly', I offer.

'In that case, you're one of the 30% of people who hate mornings.'

My brow was furrowed. The doctor was spot on. It takes three coffees before anyone's even allowed to speak to me at work.

'If you're "a bit owly" that means going to bed later and waking later provides you with the quality and quantity of sleep you need. But the world is ruled by the morning larks. These people are bright-eyed and bushy-tailed before the rest of us have rubbed the sleep from our eyes and because of that they have somehow hijacked society and imposed their preferred sleep schedules on all of us. Think about it, most employers open the doors early in the morning and most schools kick off before the children are fully awake. Life revolves around a morning lark schedule. If you're a night owl, you may be going to bed late but waking up earlier than you should. So, what happens when a night owl goes to bed at midnight but wakes up at 6am in order to shower and get to work? They lose two hours of their recommended sleep allocation, but they also lose out on an important *phase* of sleep.'

'Phase?'

'REM', explained the doctor. 'Shiny happy people, they need REM sleep, "Rapid Eye Movement". It's the deep phase of sleep. The part that cleanses your brain, helps your emotional regulation, problem solving, that kind of thing. You can shift your sleep pattern to better fit your lifestyle but these sleep tips will help, whether you're a night owl or a lark.'

I was with her, sitting upright, pencil at the ready. *Sleep tips* written as a sub-heading.

'Stick to a sleep schedule. Go to bed and wake up at the same time each day.'

'What, no lazy mid-day Sunday lie-in?'

'It throws your whole week out of kilter', she said. 'You lie in, hence you're not tired on Sunday night, so you go to bed late and Monday is off to a sleep-deprived beginning. Try this: instead of using an alarm to get out of bed in the morning, set a reminder in your smartphone to chime when it's time to *go* to bed. And, when you do, leave the phone in another room.'

I was scribbling furiously. It was all obvious but I'd clearly fallen into lazy sleep habits.

'Exercise 30 minutes each day but not too late in the day. Avoid exercise two to three hours before your bedtime. Same with caffeine and alcohol. Caffeine has a half-life of about seven hours. Have a cup of coffee at 7pm and your system still has 50% of the caffeine running around it at 2am. So no caffeine after midday and forget about decaffeinated coffee or tea, they have as much as 30% of the caffeine in regular coffee and tea. And an alcoholic nightcap may relax you but it inhibits REM sleep.'

Shiny happy people don't drink coffee after 7pm . . . I scribbled, as the doctor continued to dispense rapid-fire advice. 'Avoid large meals late at night. A large meal can cause indigestion, which interferes with sleep. And fluids, at your age, will cause you to wake up for the toilet.'

I wince at the truth of it. I sometimes toss and turn at 1am, resisting the urge to visit the bathroom. Otherwise I have to go twice, at 1am and 5am.

'Are you a napper?' she asked, ploughing on regardless. 'Because naps are double edged. A cheeky 10 minutes is restorative, but too late in the day makes it harder to fall asleep at night. Plus, if you follow all the rules you're writing down, you shouldn't be needing a catnap. Oh, and be sure to relax before bed. Give yourself a mental break at the end of each day. Remove extraneous stimulations.'

I glanced at her and she explained in plain simple English. 'Try reading or listening to music instead of watching TV or scrolling through social media. And finally', she said, 'go primitive'.

'Primitive? What, no pyjamas?' I asked, wearing my surprised eyebrows.

'No, that's commando', she corrected. 'Primitive. Sleep in a "cave". A dark, cool bedroom is a perfect environment for high-quality sleep. Eliminate the lights and sounds from smartphones, tablets, TVs, and laptops. If you use a digital alarm clock, turn it away from you so the light doesn't impact your sleep. No distractions. *BED*-room', she said, as if I was hard of hearing. 'The clue's in the name.'

The doctor stood up, her body language signalling that my 15-minute consultation was over. 'If you'll excuse me', she said, 'I've got a waiting room full of worn-down, sore-throated, swollen-glanded, flu-ridden, high-blood-pressured, near-exhausted customers. They're all in the red zone and they'll all be getting the same prescription as you.' She slid the piece of paper across the desk to me, the one word seeming kind of stark but somehow perfectly reasonable. 'Sleep', she smiled. 'Treat yourself Champ. Eight hours a night, *every* night. Give me a bell this time next week and let me know how you're getting along.'

I nodded and slipped the piece of paper into my pocket. As I turned to go she said, 'And also phone me in 50 years to let me know how you're getting along.'

'Fifty years', I laughed. 'But in 50 years I'll be . . . *106*.'

'Exactly', she said ushering me out.

I smiled my way through the waiting room, past the exhausted people awaiting their turn. I was already feeling perkier.

Phone you in 50 years? You're on![1]

---

[1]Stats for rule #8 courtesy of Matthew Walker's epic book *Why We Sleep: The New Science of Sleep and Dreams* (Penguin, 2018).

Rule #9

IT'S LOVE ACTUALLY

A real friend

the flesh & blood type!!

We rather like the song *All You Need Is Love* by the Beatles. John, Paul, Ringo, and the other chap were bang on. Love is all you need. Well, that and good coffee perhaps.

Positive psychology has a habit of taking something you always thought to be true, applying some science to it, and spewing out results that prove you were right all along.

For example, apply the magical suffix 'ology' to the subject of 'friends and family'. That sounds more sciency. Friends-and-familyology. Okay, maybe not.

But guess what? Having strong personal relationships is good for your happiness and wellbeing.

I mean, *who knew*?

In fact, so much so that it protects your health as much as quitting smoking and a great deal more than exercising. Research has shown that socially isolated people are more than twice as likely to die from heart disease as those with a solid social circle. Indeed, *'Strong social relationships support mental health, and that ties into better immune function, reduced stress and less cardiovascular activation'*, says Dr Debra Umberson, a sociologist from the University of Texas.

So friendships will boost your health and happiness but, unfortunately, many of us don't have enough of them. Several decades ago social scientists started to ask questions that gauged how many people you could turn to in a crisis, or when something really good happens to you. Their very simple question is: *'How many confidants do you have?'*

When they started doing the study several decades ago, the average number of close friends an American had was three. By 2004, the most common answer was none.

In the latest survey, the most common answer is still 'none', with men especially bad at keeping and cultivating friendships.

Which gets us scratching our heads. How can it be that in an era of digital connectivity, loneliness hangs over our culture like second-hand smoke? Once again, science has the answer – it's not the 'friends' orbiting at the farthest reaches of your Wi-Fi galaxy that matter when it comes to your health and happiness. The vital friendships – the flesh and blood ones you hug, laugh, banter, celebrate, and commiserate with – are the ones who have the greatest impact on your health and happiness.

> *'I want to be the reason you look down at your phone and smile. Then walk into a pole.'*
> *– Unknown*

Dr Robin Dunbar is an evolutionary psychologist at the University of Oxford, and someone who's had a number named after him which means he's got to be worth listening to. The 'Dunbar number' is 150, which is the approximate size of a person's social circle, or the group of friends and family members that you would invite to a large party.

Don't stress if you haven't got 150. Personally, I haven't got anywhere near that many. Remember, it's approximate. Dunbar's wider point is that your brain can't hold a close connection with more than 150. And there's more! Within that group, your closest 15 relationships, including family members or 'kin', seem to be most crucial when it comes to your mental and physical health. Your kin are those who are likely to be there when you need help.

And if we go a teenie bit further, the science once again nails a point that is intuitively obvious. Within your 15 'kin', you need between three and five proper friends for optimal wellbeing. These are your lifers, with you through thick and thin.

> *'The only way to have a friend is to be one.'*
>
> – *Ralph Waldo Emerson*

Which brings us kicking and screaming out of the scientific world into the real one. Pouli belongs to 'The Antler Club', a group of a dozen fraternity brothers that met in 1980 and have been inseparable ever since. Any excuse for a meeting will do. The longest running event in the club is Greek Thanksgiving, a completely made-up holiday which occurs on the Saturday before American Thanksgiving. Pouli is Greek and he describes this fabricated holiday as similar to the American version but with lamb shish kebabs and baklava.

We are delighted to report that even though it's not actually an official thing, Greek Thanksgiving has been running uninterrupted in the Boston area for nearly 40 years.

If you talk to Pouli he swears he's a lucky man when it comes to having such a close set of lifelong friends, but if we look a bit closer it may be the other way around. He's playing by the scientific rules above. Pouli has created his good fortune by *working hard* to stay socially connected. Note, we emphasized *working hard* because it takes effort to stay in touch. The Antler Club gatherings happen several times a year and between times they stay in touch, commiserate, celebrate, share new stories of family joys and sorrows, and rehash tales of their glory days when they all had full heads of hair and all their natural joints.

So there you have it. Positive psychology brings proof to a concept that never needed proving in the first place. Mates, pals, squad, team, tribe, gang, clan, coterie, entourage, or Antler Club. No matter what you call it, your circle of friends is critical to your happiness and your health.

So here are some gentle reminders that will boost your own happiness as well as that of those closest to you:

1. Put some work into reviving your lapsed friendships. Or, go out and find some new social connections. Instead of comparing your life to someone else's on social media, reconnect with old friends over social media. Or, look for groups of people interested in the same things you are interested in, whether that is Star Trek, Star Wars, fountain pens, quilting, quidditch, footy, football, or cricket.
2. Get out and volunteer for some cause or organization you care about. Over two-thirds of volunteers report their loneliness decreased to much healthier levels usually associated with happily married couples. Volunteering is also a scalable activity; the more you volunteer, the more new friends you'll

collect. The best side effect is that you can ward off cognitive decline in your later years.

3. Send one text or email to a different friend each day. Say hello, check in and see how they are doing, or thank them for some recent or past kindness.

4. Scroll through those digital photos you've been hoarding on your hard drive or smartphone. Find an old photo of you and an old friend you've lost touch with. Send the photo to them to spark some nostalgic reminiscing.

5. Schedule time with friends on your calendar. When there is a doubt about whether or not you can all get together, put it on all your calendars and understand you can all cancel if necessary. Most people feel the pressure of obligation to show up if it's on their calendar and know many others are expecting you to show up.

6. Staring at your phone when you get on an elevator or stand in a queue at the coffee shop signals to the rest of the world that you're avoiding eye contact and would rather not engage in any sort of interaction. But isolation is a killer, so put your smartphone in your pocket, look up, smile, and say 'hello' to a stranger. Research has shown that this simple act of human connection will raise your happiness and make you feel more connected to your community. And you never know where that simple act of connection can take you.

Rule #10

LISTEN TO UNDERSTAND, NOT TO REPLY – THEN REPLY

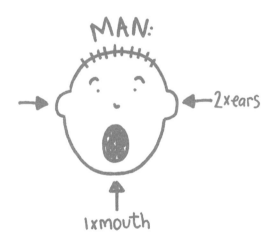

> **Clever Thought for the Day:**
> *I've taken a vowel of silnce.*

We are orators.

It's never been easier to talk, to puff ourselves up and brag about our goals and achievements. What used to be the preserve of rock stars and cult leaders is now available to us all. We are able to stand tall on our social media platforms and shout to our followers.

Now more than ever, our culture fans the flames of ego. We know, because we're guilty too!

Anyone can talk about him- or herself. By the age of seven a child has learned how to gossip and backbite.

So, what is scarce and rare? *Silence*, that's what. The ability to deliberately keep yourself out of the conversation and subsist without its validation. Indeed, we dare to venture further by posing this question: *could it be that in a shouty world, silence is the respite of the confident and the strong?*

Sanj is one-third of your author tag team. He's young, smiley, and although his skin is brown, he's a bit green in terms of life experience. But here's something he learned straight after leaving uni . . .

Talk about living the dream. I was lucky enough to spend some time living in Dubai. Picture the scene: aged 23, working in the Financial Centre, wearing a swanky suit and mirror shades. I was rubbing shoulders with people from across the world, surrounded by fancy restaurants and even fancier cars.

The first year was full of exploration. I met so many people – amazing ones, generous types, party animals, serious folk, and a variety of characters from all walks of life. I didn't connect with them all, but I noticed a common factor in those with whom I bonded. They were empathetic. They made time to listen to me – they wanted to understand my thoughts and feelings before taking the conversation further.

They listened. On reflection, it was as if the fact they were interested in me somehow made *them* more interesting.

The most interesting was 70+ Ashok, an Indian I met at the airport in Mumbai the year before. Once or twice a month I would visit Ashok and his wife and we'd spend a good few hours together – him listening to me, and me attempting to listen back. We didn't go clubbing. We didn't do fancy-pants restaurants. And yet my time with Ashok and his wife is my most treasured.

Ashok taught me the value of listening to understand. By 'taught' I don't mean he sat down and instructed me in the principles of listening, he taught by doing.

At the tender age of 23, my learning was twofold. First, if you want to build a solid relationship then you must take that time to listen to understand first. Give the other person the time and space to be able to share their thoughts and feelings with you, and once you have understood (and if you've not understood, ask for clarification) you will be able to add value to the conversation with your own viewpoint. I guess it's the old adage about having two ears and one mouth.

Second, be *genuinely* interested in people. Not pretence or fakery, it has to be a true interest in the other person. That leads you to ask real questions that take their stories further and, by spooky coincidence, they will deem you to be more interesting (which is odd because you will hardly have spoken!).

Dr Andy says this is a Dale Carnegie principle from the 1940s or, more recently, a re-telling of David Taylor's quote: *Wisdom has two parts: 1) Having a lot to say, and 2) Not saying it.*

But I don't care who wrote about it first, in terms of fanning the flames of a rock-solid relationship, listening just works.

Imagine if, instead of shouting, we all listened a whole lot better. Instead of asking depressed people 'What's the matter with you', doctors would ask 'What matters *to* you?' I'll leave you to imagine what would happen if we could get to the bottom of that.

Parents, here are some lessons from Dr Shelly Gable, who has linked listening with celebration. She suggests there are four types of response when you hear some good news.

Imagine, for example, at the dinner table, your child announces that they've got down to the final three in the auditions for the lead role in the school play. Here are the four responses in table form:

	Passive	**Active**
Constructive	*'That's great news, and about time. They should have given you a chance ages ago.'*	*'That's amazing. How do you feel? How did they tell you? How did you react? Tell me more . . .'*
Destructive	*'Oh, can you pass the salt?'*	*'Yikes. The pressure! What if you don't get it?'*

I'm hoping you are already avoiding the passive/destructive!

But look at the active/constructive, it's genius. We're not suggesting an over-the-top punching-of-the-air celebration for every smidgeon of good news, but a raising of your levels of enthusiasm means that you won't miss out on so many glorious relationship-building opportunities.

To be active/constructive you need to listen. And we mean *really* listen. Because when you understand, you can ask some more.

To be able to listen at ninja level, it helps to adopt some of the principles from coaching. Obviously, coaching is a book in its own right but we love the snazzy, slightly quirky approach of Michael Bungay-Stanier. In his marvellous book, his coaching questions are:

1. Kickstart question: What's on your mind?
2. AWE question: And what else?
3. Focus question: What's the real challenge here for you?
4. Foundation question: What do you want?
5. Lazy question: How can I help?
6. Strategic question: If you're saying yes to this, what are you saying no to?
7. Learning question: What was most useful for you?

Or, to unstick people, try the most powerful subconscious question in the world, *'If you did know the answer, what would it be?'*

Then shut up and listen while they solve the problem themselves!

Of course, as with all the other 'rules' in this book, just because it's common sense doesn't mean it's common practice. Listening is something you can get better at. So keep prodding yourself to shut up and listen. In fact, next time you're in a meeting or chatting to a colleague or at home with your family, dare to ask yourself this: *am I listening, or am I just waiting to speak?*

Rule #11

WHICHEVER GOD YOU FOLLOW, KINDNESS IS THE BEST RELIGION

> **A Thought of the Times:**
>
> *Remember, back in the day before smartphones and computers?*
> *When we used to talk to each other?*
> *F***ing awful wasn't it!*

Here, in no particular order, are 10 things that require zero talent or money. We're introducing them right now, so we can come back to them in a page or two:

1. Being on time
2. Working hard
3. Being super kind
4. Smiling
5. Good manners
6. Respect for people, things, and Mother Earth
7. Doing extra
8. Being prepared
9. A positive attitude
10. Being a nice human being

They're all great but we'd like to take a few minutes to unpick #3 because although we call ourselves 'humankind', sometimes our kindness halos can slip. The milk of human kindness can feel, at best, a bit semi-skimmed.

We three authors are all deeply into personal development, a genre often known as 'self-help'. Our book is jostling for shelf space in a crowded marketplace. Bookshops have entire sections devoted to self-help, which got us wondering if the genre has accidentally diverted itself down a cul-de-sac.

'Self-help' is all well and good, but why is there no section on 'helping others'?

The reason there is no section on 'helping others' is because it would consist of just one book and one rule.

This one and this one!

Some scene-setting for a story from author Sanj: I grew up in Neath, South Wales, at a time when there were no other brown faces (other than my mum and dad, obviously). Although Sikh by default, I did what all the white kids did. I rocked up at school, played rugby (even though cricket is in my DNA), gained a Welsh accent, went to the same lessons, and sang the Lord's Prayer in school assembly.

The only thing that was different was the way I looked. In fact, the only time in my entire childhood I realized I was 'different' was when all the kids had to draw a self-portrait in art. While 32 of my classmates squabbled over the pink pencil, I had the brown one all to myself.

Fast forward to college and I made my first brown friend, 'Dyno Dave'. Imagine the excitement! We bonded over similar family structures, a love of cricket, our genius at maths, our parents' desire for us to be engineers/doctors/accountants, and our 'tiger moms' (yes, the stereotype is alive and well in my house).

Once we'd gotten the niceties out of the way, my next question was about Dyno's name. The South Asian tradition is to have a proper Indian name – your actual real name – and then an English version that white people can pronounce.

'It's "Dave"', said Dyno Dave. 'Sure the "Dyno" bit is a nickname but my name's David. *Dave.*' This revelation that Dave's actual real name was 'Dave' turned my world upside down. Not only was Dave the first brown person I'd ever met, at age 18, I'd met a breed of person I never imagined existed, a brown Christian. I mean, who knew?

It was a complete eye-opener – people might not actually be who we think they are – and from that point onwards I saw everything and everyone differently. In a weird turn of events, instead of looking at people's differences, I started to spot their similarities.

Fast forward to age 23. I moved to Dubai. Remember, I'm from Neath in South Wales. In case you've never been to Neath let me paint a picture for you. First, imagine the glass and steel skyscrapers of Dubai. Then imagine they've all been knocked down and someone has grassed the entire area and put sheep on it. And climate change has resulted in Dubai becoming cold and very, very wet. Next you have to imagine that Dubai has loosened its alcohol laws so there are lots of pubs. In which the men sing a lot. The women just drink.

Got the picture? Good, because that's Neath, and Dubai was the *exact opposite.*

Day 1 in the ever-so-fancy Dubai International Financial Centre office, I found myself with a young woman from Saudi Arabia to my right (Sunni Muslim), Ranim from Syria on my left (Shia Muslim), two women from Lebanon ahead (Maronite Catholic and Armenian Apostolic), and Riku a middle-aged Japanese guy behind (Shinto). And me, a confused Sikh/Church of Wales hybrid, suddenly immersed in the world's spiciest cultural diversity melting pot.

Different races, customs, colours, education, language, and traditions thrown together. And when you boil all the froth off the cultural melting pot you are left with the essence of humanity. The good stuff distilled into the goo at the bottom of the diversity pan – the common denominator across all the wonderful people I met was . . .

. . . no, it wasn't our clothes or language and certainly not our various gods.

It was kindness.

We each followed a different deity and yet all our religions pointed to kindness.

So did our instincts.

Kindness is at our core. Kindness is us at our best. Kindness is what lifts us to a life of service. Kindness creates (and nourishes) human connection. I worked in finance but I soon learned that it wasn't money that made the world go round, it was kindness.

Full-fat human kindness.

So here are five reminders of the little things that you can do to help squeeze a pail of the full-fat good stuff from the udder of life.

1. Be kind, *quietly*, in your head.

Often forgotten in the midst of trying to be a half-decent person is the necessity to be kind to *yourself*. Catch yourself doing things well, give yourself a bit of encouragement, compliment the brilliant you on a situation well handled. We're advising that you do this quietly, in your head, because an out-loud *'Oh my goodness, how epic am I, being confident enough to speak up in a business meeting'* can sound a bit narcissistic.

Remember, your brain is organized in the exact opposite way. Its pre-programmed bias towards negativity gives you a running commentary on what an idiot you are and how you handled the situation badly. *'Oh my goodness, what an idiot I am for pretending to be confident enough to speak up in a business meeting'* is a more likely internal dialogue.

It's worth remembering that just because you've messed up doesn't mean you *are* messed up! When you err, give yourself a break. Let compassion soothe your pain. Instead of beating yourself up, be supportive and acknowledge that you have tried your best, that you had good intentions, and that you have a good heart.

Being kind to yourself is a way of rewiring your thinking. Yes, the old software has to be overwritten. Once again, we're not advocating an over-the-top dollop of mental kindness – you'll occasionally deserve a bit of a self-inflicted mental kicking (because you will mess up, say the wrong thing, and misjudge a situation) but we're asking that you go easy on yourself.

Kindness to others is an obvious rule. We're simply re-engineering a well-known adage: in terms of kindness we're asking you to *do unto yourself as you would do to others*.

2. Say nice things about people.

It turns out my straight-talking grandma was a bit of a guru with her adage of *'if you haven't got anything nice to say about someone, then keep your gob shut'*.

Words create worlds, so when speaking about someone, speak positively.

Here's a Sanj example. I was visiting my friend Sid and, to be honest, I was a bit nervous about meeting a new crowd of people. But Sid didn't just go through the motions of *'Everyone, this is Sanj. Sanj, this is everyone'*, he said this: *'This is Sanj, my brother from Wales who is visiting. He's a great guy. Let's make sure we show him the best time possible over the next few days.'*

It's amazing how such a small change in words had such a big impact on me. And it got me thinking I should up my game so, when the opportunity arose, I paid it forward. Sure, I stumbled a bit by introducing one of my friends as *'This is Oli, my mate from Uni'*, before quickly correcting myself and adding, *'Actually, Oli is one of my closest friends from Uni, someone I lived with for two years, one of the most talented people I know AND makes me a cake every year for my birthday!'*

The crowd grinned. There was an audible *'Cake! Wow!'* and everyone immediately wanted to chat to Oli, knowing it might lead to their very own Victoria sponge.

I've heard it called an 'emotional bucket'. We all want to feel good and it's our job to fill other people's buckets. Notice the small things. Comment on someone's lovely cardigan, happy face, smiley eyes, or positive attitude. Sure, there's a fine line to be drawn between being totally genuine or a tad over the top. We're not asking you to be creepy, salacious, smarmy, inappropriate, or politically incorrect – just, well . . . *kind*.

Genuinely and *wholeheartedly* kind.

It's a bucket-filler for them, and you!

Try this exercise. List five people in your life and write in one sentence how you would introduce them in the best way possible.

1. _____
2. _____
3. _____
4. _____
5. _____

3. Say nice things about people *behind their back.*

The 'behind their back' bit is important because it somehow supercharges your kindness. At a basic level, your nice comment is quite likely to filter back to the person you are complimenting, which makes them feel great. But at a higher level it creates what's called 'spontaneous trait transference', a phenomenon whereby all those nice qualities you mentioned about the person who's currently out of earshot get attributed to you. Yes, the person you're talking to thinks you're also nice, generous, hard-working, and kind.

As with all our 'rules', don't overdo it, and we're not asking you to be manipulative or Machiavellian either. Our challenge is for you to commit to saying nice things about the other departments in your organization, your kids, mum, partner, next-door neighbor . . . *when they're not there to hear it*.

And see what happens.

4. Practise *random* and *anonymous* acts of kindness.

So far, our kindness bucket-filling has been purely through words. But we all know that actions speak louder than words, so here's a reminder about acts of kindness that turn you into an everyday superhero. Remember our top 10 list from earlier; the list requires no talent or money so there really are no excuses.

Three points worth noting about acts of kindness. First, very small things can have a very big impact. A smile, a chat, an open door . . . make someone a cuppa, tell someone they're ace, give a hug, hold a hand, let someone into the traffic, pay a compliment . . . these acts are all emotional bucket-fillers.

Second, being kind by nature is great, but surprising yourself with your spontaneity is even better. *Random* acts of kindness are sublime because everyone wins. Setting out to be super-kind is a worthy intention, but spontaneity adds a frisson of excitement because you're never quite sure how or where your kindness superpower is going to reveal itself.

And third, to raise your frisson to full-blown giddiness, why not go for a double whammy of *anonymous random* acts of kindness. It's ninja level. Paying at the McDonalds drive-thru for the car behind you, washing the graffiti off a random wall, leaving some credit in the vending machine so the next person gets a freebie . . .

Sure, this type of kindness often requires you to part with a small amount of cash or your precious time, but it's well worth it because somebody's day is made and nobody knows it was you. It's weird, but the anonymity somehow makes your day too.

5. It doesn't matter what everyone else is doing, it matters what YOU are doing.

And our final challenge is to be a kindness ninja, even to the people who are not kind back. Because no matter how fabulous you are, there will always be the unkind humankind, the ones who do the opposite of this chapter.

For some people, negativity rules. They say horrible things about people to their face and behind their back, they criticize, they're double quick to badmouth anyone and everyone, they don't let you out in the traffic (and if you let them out they don't thank you!), and they jump the supermarket queue.

The 'busy rude' is a growing tribe whose milk of human kindness has gone a bit sour. Our tagline is this: *if you can't beat 'em, definitely don't join 'em*.

Our challenge to you is this: to be a kindness ninja you have to be super-kind to *everyone*. Yes, even the 'busy rude' and the one or two idiots who don't seem to deserve it. If they're not very nice people that's because they've not experienced enough kindness or love.

So, love the unloved, be nice to the not-so-nice, and be kind to the unkind.

In a world that is dominated by differences, let kindness be your god.

Rule #12

NUDGE
THE MACHINE

> *'If it ain't broken, break it.'*
>
> *Alex Steele*

Have you ever been the wrong way around IKEA?

If so, you're already a deviant so you can skip this rule. But if not, why not? (By the way, in case you didn't know, 'IKEA' is an old Swedish word, meaning 'a tedious walk on a long winding path'.)

Next time, we dare you to go in through the main entrance, grab your notepad and tiny pencil, and turn left. Yes, avert your eyes from the arrows on the floor, ignore the herds who've gone right, and fight your instinct to follow them.

Bear left. With confidence. It starts you at the toilets and meat-balls. Your actual shopping begins in the cushions and soft fabrics section. Now please continue that journey in your imagination. We're going to leave you on that solitary IKEA expedition and come back to you later to see how you're getting along . . .

Meantime, culture. Your need to belong is strong. Our gregarious nature means that we look at everyone else and take our cue from them. You don't know you're doing it, culture just seeps into your bone marrow. You develop an accent to fit into the community around you. You wear certain outfits to fit the situation. The wrong outfit in the wrong situation is socially awkward (for example, if you wear budgie smugglers to work they'll be whispering about you at the water cooler). I have learned that a handshake with my father-in-law has to be a five-minute bone-crunching affair with full grin and an unnerving amount of eye contact, whereas with my teenage nephews it's a hand clasp, shoulder-to-shoulder 'bro hug' and grunty *'yo'*. Eye contact is minimal because they have phone screens that need attending to. That example shows that culture changes with the generations.

Culture broadens out from individuals to society. Obesity is a classic modern example. It's often described as an 'epidemic', as in there's an outbreak of it. Which, of course, culturally there is. We see so many overweight people that it seems kind of okay. Once it's normalized it's easy to talk yourself into – *everyone else is piling on a few pounds, and 'going large', so maybe I should too* – and before you know it you too are belching your way through an unhappy meal and a gallon of Pepsi.

Tattoos, fashions, haircuts . . . we live and breathe culture without really knowing it. In the same way that fish have never realized they're in water, you're swimming so deeply in culture that you don't know you're in it. Culture is just the way things are. We're enmeshed in a matrix of language, habits, and thinking.

But, in a detour from normal personal development books, let's linger on two themes from the previous paragraph: fish and haircuts.

Specifically, the mullet, which is both.

We can learn a lot about culture from the mullet. The haircut, gosh, that says a lot about the wearer. An outbreak of mullets tells me we're somewhere in the far east of Europe where the 1980s still has a firm fashion foothold.

But learning-wise there's probably more to be gleaned from the fish. Mullet aggregate together in huge numbers, and by huge we mean HUUUUUGE. 'Chains' of mullet schools 100 km long have been seen migrating in the Caspian Sea.[1]

And as with all schools, we can learn a lot. If every fish just did its own thing there'd be chaos, so to avoid mullet mayhem the school has rules, very precise arrangements, which allow the system to maintain some semblance of order. Documentary aerial footage shown from above shows the silvery mass motoring along at a phenomenal pace. Indeed, one of the benefits of joining forces with the crowd is that the shoal can swim faster than an individual mullet. But despite its mass, the shoal of mullet can turn almost instantaneously, darting left, swishing right, or powering full steam ahead. Millions of fish in a true display of synchronized swimming.

But if you stick a documentary team *into* the water, you get a different picture. Each individual fish isn't aware that it's in a 100-km shoal. Molly Mullet isn't watching the whole shoal, she's just got her glassy eye on the fish next to her, who just happens to be Henry to her left and Elijah to her right. With Errol swimming above and Aakanksha bobbing about below. (Yes, it's a multi-cultural school.)

And Henry and Elijah have got one glassy eye on Molly and whoever else is hemming them into the shoal from their other sides. They focus on the next fish along and swim as fast as they can to keep up. *Swoosh left, swish hard right, full steam ahead . . .*

---

[1] Interestingly, this is the same area where the haircut retains a stronghold. I'm not suggesting there's causation. I'm just saying.

And, on occasion, the entire shoal will do a U-turn. Check the YouTube footage. It's something to behold.

But here's the thing. If you take a careful look at the school of mullet, you'll notice that although the fish all *appear* to be swimming in the same direction, they're actually not. In reality, at any time, there will be a small group swimming in a different direction. These brave creatures are swimming *against* the flow, *against* conventional wisdom.

As they move in another direction, they create conflict and friction, and this causes discomfort for themselves and the rest of the school. I'm guessing they get a bit bashed about. But remember, Molly, Henry, Elijah, Errol, and Aakanksha aren't watching the whole shoal, they're just doing what their neighbour does. So there comes a tipping point. When Molly sees her neighbour flip 180° she goes too, and Henry, Elijah, Errol, and Aakanksha follow. And their neighbouring mullet follow them. When the small group reaches a critical mass of truly committed mullet – not a huge number like 50 or 80%, but *2%* who are truly committed to a new direction, the rest of the school suddenly turns and goes with them – almost instantaneously!

The disruptors eventually win.

'Never doubt that a small group of thoughtful, committed citizens can change the world; indeed, it's the only thing that ever has.'

– Margaret Mead

A few paragraphs ago we left you wandering the 'wrong' way around IKEA. How's your journey going? Getting in the way probably? Sidestepping? I'm hearing a lot of *'Sorry. Excuse me.'* I'm guessing you're being bashed about by the majority who are coming right at you. It's uncomfortable.

We're wondering how many IKEA customers it would take for *everyone* to start going the 'wrong' way. That has to be an academic paper in the making. Our best guess is that if you watched three or four families in front of you go left, you'd go left too. And if you went left, the people following you would also go left.

Of course, our rule about 'nudging the machine' isn't *literally* about becoming a maverick IKEA shopper. It's to cattle-prod you into thinking about cultural habits that you might have accidentally fallen into. Habits that aren't necessarily serving you well.

Look around at the masses buzzed up on caffeine, sugar, fast food, and even faster media.

Local rules have changed. Mullet is how we *used* to be. Physical proximity was the thing. You lived in a village of 150 people – max – and you did what they did. But in the last 10 years the meaning of 'proximity' has changed. Technology has morphed us from physical proximity to social proximity. More recently warp speed has cheek-wobbled us beyond social proximity to *hyper social* connectivity.

7.5 billion mullet are now hyper socially connected to 7.5 billion mullet from across the planet.

The internet spreads news, fashions, gossip, and haircuts in double quick time. It also spreads negativity, outrage, hatred, and bile. A whole shoal of people in one region of the network starts to feel a particular emotional state at a particular time, which becomes a hashtag . . . the next time zone wakes up and logs on . . . the hashtag of negativity gets passed around the globe.

Bottom line? It's easy to fit in. You're built to fit in. And fitting in is a perfectly okay short-term strategy, but I can't think of a single person in history who has ever achieved greatness by fitting in.

Your long-term strategy should be to stand out. For the *right* reasons.

We called this rule 'nudge the machine'. What we didn't tell you upfront is that *YOU ARE THE MACHINE*. In which case, maybe it's less about following the mullet and more about setting an amazing example which some may call 'leadership'. We're not asking you to be Martin Luther King or Gandhi. But somebody, somewhere, has to be the catalyst for a better way of thinking and behaving. A more POSITIVE way of thinking and behaving. A spreader of uplifting messages, good news, and compliments. A hashtag that brings some happiness.

If you're that person, Molly, Henry, Elijah, Errol, and Aakanksha might follow. And if they follow, their followers might follow . . .

And 7.5 billion human beings might turn in an instant.

Rule #13

YOUR HAPPINESS IS BIGGER THAN YOU

> Thought for the Day:
>
> *You don't need a certain number of friends. You just need a number of friends you can be certain of.*

There are four types of human energy: physical, mental, emotional, and relational – only one of which is renewable.

Physical energy is the body's naturally occurring energy, produced by burning calories. If you need more physical energy, you need to consume more calories. But beware, fast food fills you up without nourishing you and energy drinks make you alert without energizing you. It pays to consume the right kind of calories.

Mental energy is specifically to do with mental concentration and brain work. There's a psychological state of flow (see rule #17), the sweet spot when you are challenged in just the way you want to be challenged. Boom, you're in the zone and are so engrossed in the task that time hurtles by. Such is your absorption that you might accidentally skip a meal without noticing. Crucially, when you're in the state of flow you don't feel weary or exhausted. You feel amazing!

It's a great state to aim for, but most people experience the opposite. You can't get going, you procrastinate, multi-task, flit around, grab a coffee, check Facebook . . . your psychological energy tank dries up as your day drags by.

Emotional energy is all about experiencing intense feelings and is depleted by, for example, periods of intense excitement or sadness. The more intense the emotion, the more draining it can become. Extreme sadness is hard work. Grief drains you. But even extreme highs aren't sustainable. Think back to how exhausted you felt after attending a joyous wedding.

But it's the last one that's our focus. *Relational* energy, in contrast to the other three, is an energy that increases as it is exercised. This form of energy is enhanced and revitalized through positive interpersonal relationships. Relational energy is uplifting, invigorating, rejuvenating – and where does 'relational energy' come from?

People, that's where.

It's perfectly possible for people to receive an energy transfusion and, what's more, this renewable human energy is clean and totally free.

Got that? Good, because it's the scaffolding that helps us build the next point . . .

It's not just your energy that's transferable. Emotions are viral too. Your emotional system is an open loop so, in Wi-Fi terms, everyone can log onto your signal and you can log onto theirs. No passwords required! So, when you're feeling great, other people will catch that feeling. If you're having a stinker, guess what, you're contaminating those around you with toxic feelings.

The openness of your emotional system, the fact that we're hard-wired to catch other people's feelings, means that we create one another. That sentence has such huge connotations that it probably needs unpicking. Your emotions not only affect *you* and the chemical composition of *your* body, they also transmit to those around you, creating *that* person in *that* moment.

You might need to re-read the previous paragraph and let its enormity sink in. It boils down to this: *you are playing an active part in making or breaking other people's days*. It works via mirror neurons, which means we're compelled to copy others' emotions and behaviours. These mirror neurons allow contagion, letting the feelings we witness flow through us, thus helping us get in sync with the person feeling the emotion. This ability to 'feel' *with* and *for* them is the basis of empathy.

Remember, humans are constructed with this emotional openness. It's built in as part of your operating system – factory fitted. You can't remove it.

But you can *upgrade* it.

To explain it properly, we need to go back in time. Human beings are gregarious, we're pack animals. We always have been and we always will be. Stated as simply as possible it means this: human beings need other human beings. You need to belong to a tribe. Think about it. Way way *waaaay* back, your tribe kept you physically safe. Your fellow villagers looked out for you. Your tribe fought against other tribes, defending your territory and life. Hunting a wild boar on your own was fruitless – you'd die of hunger very quickly – but as a team, with one group beating the earth to spook the hog in your direction, bringing home the bacon was not guaranteed, but a lot more likely.

Other than keeping you relatively safe and well fed, the tribe also kept you mentally and emotionally healthy. Tucking into your hog roast, followed by all that dancing round the campfire, was calorifically, socially, and emotionally nutritious.

If you don't believe me, on December 25th, experiment with Christmas on your own. Pull a cracker, you against you. Wear the silly hat, read the joke to yourself, eat a microwaved turkey dinner, and play Solitaire in the solitary confinement of your kitchen. I guarantee you'll find it joyless, pointless, and thoroughly depressing.

So, for your physical and *emotional* wellbeing, you need to be connected to a tribe. And for a modern-day 'tribe' read family, work team, WhatsApp group, street gang, orchestra, half mara-thoners, Twitter followers, fellow backpackers, football team supporters, Trekker convention crowd, gym bunnies, or weight watchers on a Tuesday night.

The world has moved on from our hunter-gatherer days. Despite what you see on the news, *physically* we've never been safer. You no longer need to belong to a social group to guarantee your physical safety, but the need for social interaction remains. *Mentally* and *emotionally* we still need to connect with a tribe. It transpires that human emotions have a collective existence and not just an individual existence. They also pass through genera-tions like an invisible thread in what Eckhart Tolle calls the 'pain body'. For example, the emotional effects of slavery are still being felt by today's descendants.

It's powerful stuff.

If you sat down and mapped your social network it'd be messy. There'd be a dense knit of ties in the middle (this will be a cluster of people you see frequently; close family, besties, work col-leagues, etc,) with a thinning out towards the edge (relatives you see once in a blue moon, customers you visit annually) and those right on the periphery of your social network (for example, the lady on the checkout who you might only ever meet once).

It's not unlike Christmas tree lights. When I'm doing the tree, the lights start off in a pile on the floor, awaiting their untanglement and drapery. I plug them in, with fingers crossed that they still work after 350 dormant days. *Phew!* They illuminate in a satisfying messy mass of colour with a big knot in the middle and then a thinning of lights at the edge.

Imagine every light is a person in your life, and all the wires between them are your social ties. But it's *your* personal network so *you* are slap bang in the middle of the illuminated spaghetti.

It doesn't take too much effort to imagine you on a good day versus you on a rotten one. How many lights can you light up, or switch off? That's worth mulling over for a while.

Remember those pesky mirror neurons from a few paragraphs ago? Emotional contagion works on the outside *and* the inside. If one person gets angry then others will mimic their angry face. But your outward display also influences your inner state. In *Toy Story*, when Mr Potato Head puts his angry eyes on, he *becomes* angry.

Thankfully, it works with smiles too. When someone smiles because they feel happy, you mimic the smile and also feel happy. So, far from other people not being able to make us feel anything, we are in fact hard-wired in ways that predispose us to feel others' joy and pain. Basically, you cannot NOT have an impact!

While we cannot force people to be positive, we can plant seeds. It is truly a case of leading by example. Your attitudes and behaviours are infectious. I guess the million-dollar double-barrelled question is: *who* will you 'emotionally infect' and *what* will you 'infect' them with?

Renowned scientists Nicholas Christakis and James Fowler report that a happy friend makes you 25% happier (but only if they live within a mile of you), a happy brother or sister raises your happiness by 14%, and a happy neighbour raises your happiness by a whopping 34%.

But there's more! Emotions have a 'hyper-dyadic spread' – they pass from person to person, *beyond* an individual's direct social ties. Your 'emotional spillage' creates a ripple effect that reaches three degrees of people removed from you, meaning you are affecting your friends, your friends' friends, and your friends' friends' friends.

Here are the important numbers:[1] 16, 10, and 6.

Imagine you've got a smile on your face and a positive attitude. Everyone with whom you come into *direct* contact experiences an emotional uplift of 16%. Remember, these are your regular face-to-face contacts; your nearest and dearest. You light up those closest to you by a minimum of 16%.

But it doesn't stop there.

Those 16% happier folk then pass on their happiness to everyone they encounter, raising *their* levels by 10%. You haven't actually met these ten-percenters directly, but they have caught your happiness indirectly. The entire middle mass of Christmas tree lights is now illuminated.

And, to complete the ripple, these 10% happier folk pass your happiness on to everyone *they* meet by an extra 6%. The Christmas tree lights on the periphery are now glowing too.

[1]Christakis, N. and Fowler, J. (2011) *Connected: The Amazing Power of Social Networks and How They Shape our Lives.* Harper Press.

How many people do you come into direct contact with every single day? Let me do the sums for you: at a conservative estimate, let's assume you meet three people at home, 15 work colleagues, three people in the supermarket queue, a shop assistant, the lady behind the counter at the petrol station, plus you smile at five random strangers . . . that's 28 people that you've come into direct contact with.

For the sake of simplicity, let's assume that they also meet 28 people and those 28 also meet 28.

Your happiness has therefore leaked out of you and rippled to 21,952 people. And that's a *conservative* estimate! If you're in a 'people job' such as teaching, nursing, or sales, you are meeting many more than 28 people so your sphere of influence is jaw-dropping.

The Christmas tree lights are ablaze. Because *you* lit them! But remember, each of those Christmas tree lights has its own network, equally as messy as yours. You, on a good day, have helped spark light into their network too.

But beware! The ripple also works with negativity. And remember, it's far easier to be negative. This positive malarkey is a learned behaviour. It takes commitment and a little effort.

It boils down to this. If you need to change your attitude, then do so. Nobody's going to do it for you. If you can't be bothered to be happy for yourself, cultivate it for those closest to you.

Be the light! Get bothered for THEM!

And to help you light up your network, here are some how-tos.

First up, doors. The Doors had a hit song called 'Light my fire' which we'd like to unpick. But in a delicious deviation from other personal development we don't want to focus on the lyric, that'd be too obvious/easy. We want to home in on the door bit.

Yes, doors. The *importance* of doors.

Every door is an opportunity to make an entrance. Literally! Every door you walk through is an opportunity to recalibrate yourself. A chance to adjust your posture, walk a wee bit taller and with a degree more confidence. Every door is a chance to adjust your face, possibly deciding to turn your mouth up at the corners.

Once again, we're recommending that you do this sensibly and within the parameters of reasonable human behaviour. To be clear, if you bounce through every door with jazz hands, an inane grin, and *'Ta-daaaa, here I am you lucky people!'* you'll get a punch on the nose. (Remember the grinogogs from earlier? Their fakery makes you want to do them some physical harm.)

We're talking about starting a new habit of sharing positivity more frequently and consistently. The best way to create a new habit is to tie the new habit (smiling) to an existing trigger (walking through a door).

Rather than overdoing it, we want you to train yourself to enter every door with a modicum of normality, but dare to push towards the upper end of the energy spectrum. Walk tall, smile, and recalibrate towards confidence. If you're going to be in the room, *be* in the room. And, yes, *every single door*. Even when walking into an empty room. Remember, your external body language (your smile, posture, and confidence) affects your internal state. So, at the very least, it's a chance for you to upgrade that lazy body language to something more energetic. Basically, if you walk tall and smile, *you'll* feel a whole lot better.

The rub being the 16, 10, and 6 percentages from earlier. If you get it right (and we appreciate you won't always), you've provided a spark for others. You've lit up this particular room and can now wear the smug smile of satisfaction that you've created a chain reaction.

Rule #14
BE MORE DOG

"life is like a
box of chocolates,
er actually -
a bowl of water,
woof!"

Your first Spot the Dog book, re-imagined:

See Spot run.

See Spot jump.

See Spot viciously attack Rover over a bowl of dog food.

'Be more dog' is a fabulous rule that works on so many levels. We could have written this rule to be about loyalty, friendship, or how a dog somehow manages to get excited every single day. Or we could have just asked you to be the kind of person your dog *thinks* you are – which, in one word, is *AMAZING!*

Your dog loves you. Unconditionally.

But no. All of the above fall into the realm of the bleedin' obvious and in the interests of creating new rules for a new world, we thought we'd take another angle: dog fighting.

I've owned dogs longer than I've had kids and longer than I've been married so trust me, I know how to *accidentally* start a fight between two dogs who otherwise get along well. Simply place a single bowl of food between two or three hungry dogs and watch the drama unfold. In an effort to establish their claim on the food, dogs will snarl, bark, and sometimes even attack each other.

But here's the funny thing about dogs: they have short memories when it comes to these types of seemingly life-and-death struggles. Just minutes after breaking up this kind of food fight, my three dogs will all have their collective snouts buried in a bowl of water with tongues flailing and drops of water flying everywhere as they communally quench their thirsts with not a growl or snarl to be heard.

At each other's throats one minute and happily playing ball the next?

What gives?

Dogs that fight over bowls of food, table scraps, or poorly thrown dog treats are feeling a sense of scarcity. Most dog owners feed their pets on some sort of schedule, especially if there is more than one dog in the home. That means dogs learn that the food is available in limited quantities during limited periods of time. It becomes a zero-sum game between them. They feel the urge to get as much as they can, even if it means fighting their litter-mates. They probably fear that food might not be available again for a long time. This is a very primitive, scarcity mentality.

On the other hand, most dog owners leave water bowls out all day long with the water replenished often. The dogs feel no sense of scarcity when it comes to drinking water. And besides, it's tasteless and lukewarm, not some feast that smells of beef, or chicken, or fish.

In other words, water is in abundance.

And guess what? People also have issues with scarcity and abundance. Just listen to what people complain about the most and it's likely to be about what they *don't* have: money, love, power, time, talent, or freedom.

Tens of thousands of years ago, humans learned that food, shelter, and safety were scarce. Because, back then, they were! We evolved to notice the areas in our lives where we lacked rather than the areas where we were overstocked. That scarcity hangover affects us today.

Our fear of scarcity often manifests in feelings of envy. Envy can damage your sense of abundance and it can begin at an early age. Have you ever witnessed young siblings comparing the size of a slice of cake they have each received? They get out their micrometer and measure the slice that mum or dad has handed them to ensure they both received equal portions. That's 'early onset envy' and it can continue to plague you into adulthood. I've overhead billionaire tech entrepreneurs comparing the size of their . . . private jets.

Envy is hard to avoid in the day and age of social media. We are constantly bombarded with images of our friends' 'highlight reels' on Facebook, Snapchat, Twitter, and Instagram. We see the fabulous vacations, the second and third homes, the new cars, the wonderfully successful offspring, the perfect spouses, and the endless stream of carefully collated images to present their absolute best side to the world. Our brains don't pause to realize these are just the highlights of their lives.

And we compound the problem by comparing their highlight reel to an *average* day in our lives. We fall into a trap of feeling like we haven't been successful enough, haven't done enough in our lives, have failed our children, and have disappointed our parents. It's a constant battle to find some sense of abundance while experiencing FOMO.

The difference between feeling scarcity and feeling abundance is simply a shift in your mindset. Two people, in completely identical situations, can have opposite reactions and feelings.

It's like the classic rabbit/duck optical illusion (see Figure 14.1). It's the same bunch of lines and cross hatching but one person's interpretation is completely different from the other.

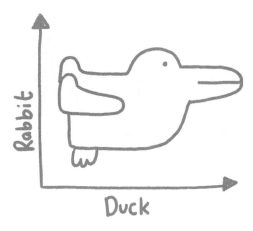

Figure 14.1 *The rabbit/duck optical illusion.*

There are best-selling books about 'abundance'. For what it's worth, we're not really into visualizing a lottery win as a way of attracting it into your life. Same with the Ferrari or your dream job. Visualizing might work, but it smacks of desperation.

But it's perfectly possible to redirect your thinking towards an abundance mindset. Here are a few starters:

1. Remember when you left school/college, what did you earn? What do you earn now?
2. Do you remember when you desperately wanted what you currently have?
3. What possessions do you currently have that you wanted years ago?
4. When you were at school, what places did you really want to visit? What places have you visited in the last 10 years?
5. What relationships did you want to develop years ago?
6. What career did you want to have?

7. Make a list of every personal and professional accomplishment you have ever achieved. Shoot for 50 items or more on the list. (You'll be amazed at how much you've achieved and you'll be impressed with your ability to persevere in difficult situations.)
8. Stop comparing yourself to other people. Start comparing yourself to who you were yesterday, last year, or a decade ago.
9. List three things that have made you smile in the last 24 hours.
10. What three things have you learnt in the past month?
11. What three aspects of your life are going in the right direction?
12. Try changing 'I didn't have time' for 'I didn't make time'.

And remember: life is like a ~~box of chocolates~~ bowl of water, not a bowl of dog food!

Rule #15

YOUR SMARTPHONE IS MAKING YOU STUPID

"We can't Sleep together anymore!"

Health warning!
Watching porn can give you a very unrealistic view of sex. I, for instance, have always regretted not becoming a washing machine repairman.

Dear Smartphone

Please excuse my clumsy language. This has been such a hard letter to write.

It's safe to say we've been through thick, thin, and everything in between. You need to understand that I love you. I always have and I always will. You are my Swiss Army Knife of communication.

But after being together for more than 20 years, I'm going to have to walk away.

Wowza, what adventures we've had! Remember when we met all those years ago? There was nothing smart about you back then, not even a camera or touchscreen. But you were gorgeous with your clunky buttons and tiny green and black screen. We made some *actual* phone calls and played Snakes together.

They were such joyous times, way before social media and 18-month contracts. You'd sit alongside my camera, Kodi, because I needed you both! *Imagine?*

Hey, speaking of which, have you ever spared a thought for old Kodi. It's such a long time ago, I bet you've forgotten. Me, you, and him, we used to hang around together. It was before selfies had been invented. Kodi had a film and you'd have to wind him on. And there was no looking at what you'd taken and deleting the dodgy ones. The old fella would cough up his 24 or 36 roll, we'd toddle off to the chemist – yes, *the chemist* – and come back two weeks later to see what Kodi had managed to capture.

Obviously, he's gone now. I've had to retire the old boy. He just couldn't compete with your new triple lens. I've put him in a drawer, along with all the other things you've made obsolete; torch, diary, alarm clock, radio, maps, and calculator.

And yet somehow, over the past 10 years something's not felt right. You've changed. Your size has been all over the place for starters. You started big, then went tiny, then you went through a flip phase, and now you've ballooned again. It must be all that all-you-can-eat data. Bingeing's not good for you. Your screen is massive! And, of course, you've glammed up, all swanky full colour and swipey.

Our relationship's become complicated. *You've* become complicated! Plus, you never leave me alone. All those reminders, emails, notifications, and WhatsApp groups. And your constant buzzing. Even in the night! These last few years you've become a bit needy!

We used to be besties, joined at the hip. *Literally*, with you snuggled in my pocket. And now you're in my hand, almost permanently. I've no idea how many times I catch your eye, but I glance a lot. I know I do! It's a reflex action, checking if you've lit up with something.

Anything!

But the worst bit is that as you've changed, you've changed *me*. And not for the better, I might add. You bring out the worst in me. In fact – and please keep this to yourself – I'm not sure I like me anymore.

Cutting to the chase, there's only so long that I can stay in an abusive relationship. Yes, we've had good times, I'm not denying that your camera roll has some corkers on it. And we've done some epic selfies. But my relationship with you has been so full-on that I've neglected the important people in my life. I sit in the same room as them but I'm not *with* them, I'm with you: scrolling, swiping, double-thumbing, liking, poking, commenting, checking, following, un-following. And when I'm with you, I'm *absent* from them.

And that's not right or fair.

It's not just at home. When I'm at the cinema, I'm with you, scrolling during the slow bits. I'm with you in a traffic jam, checking if there's a quicker route. We're even together in the toilet! (I've dropped you in twice, sorry about that!)

The final straw was when I noticed you were trying to wheedle into my baby niece's life. She's five months old for heaven's sake! And already she's wanting to hold you, touch you, scroll you, chew you . . . like I say, your neediness has become a bit of an issue.

Me and thee, sometimes we can spend a whole eight hours together. That's 50% of my entire waking hours. Half my actual life. And when I'm with you, it's not that I've put time on hold. When I put you face down an hour of my actual real life has passed by. Or two hours. Or three. I'm not going to get those hours back. I've frittered them away. And recently I started to add up the hours and it made me scared.

Scared of the things I haven't done, the sights I didn't see, the moments that passed me by, and the people I neglected to spend time with. Those Twitter followers are all well and good. Those FB friends are lovely and I adore my Instagrammers. But I need to commit time to the *real* people in my life. The flesh and blood ones. Those closest to me. Those who often sit in the same room as me, thumbing their phones while I thumb you.

I'm breaking up with you so I can commit to them.

And while I'm at it, there's one more thing. You're a smartphone, right? I get that you've got Google built in and the entire contents of the world is available through you. But your smartness is making me dumb. I don't think anymore. I don't debate because, what's the point when I just Google the answer?

And, dear Smartphone, you are such a time-waster! I was with you on the Midland Mainline Derby to St Pancras last Monday and I watched three episodes of Friends from 1995. On your miserable cracked, peeling screen.

Why?

Why did you make me do that?

I saw them in actual 1995! If you hadn't been there I would have just stared out of the window, or read a book, or people watched, or dreamed, or watched the sheep, or chatted to the young lady opposite and accidentally met the love of my life. All those missed opportunities! BECAUSE OF YOU!

And I don't want this to be a character assassination, but you might need to take a good long hard look at yourself and what you've become – an all-consuming attention-seeking flirt. A pic-teaser. *Look at me! Let me show you this! Look at this funny cat!* Ultimately, it's your possessiveness that's driven me away. You're controlling, and I need to do something to wrestle my life back.

So I'm proposing that we cool it. As I said at the outset, it's not lack of love. I love you. I'll always love you, but I need some time and space to get my head together. I'm suggesting we cut down our time together by 75%.

Yes, that's *three-quarters* in olden language.

I already know I'll miss you and I'm certain to be tempted, so it's got to be mutual. You've got to agree to me switching off *all* notifications and *all* alerts, deleting a swathe of apps, living 75% in airplane mode, and . . .

. . . I'm not sure how to say this . . .

. . . *we can't sleep together anymore*.

No more between the sheets action. That bit's over for good. I'm so sorry. I can actually feel tears welling. You're going to have to agree to sleep on the sofa or in the spare room. If you prefer, I can put you in the drawer with Kodi and the gang? You can't be the last thing I see at night and the first thing my bleary eyes lock onto in the morning. It's not healthy.

You say you're all about freedom, but you're not. I feel trapped.

You say you're all about connection, but you're not. I feel lonely.

I've got a life that needs living, *fully*. That means I'm truly committed to less *you* time and more *me* time. Because I know that a better me is the key to better relationships with my family and friends.

Thanks for the memories.

x

Rule #16
DITCH THE SUPERHERO CLICHÉ

Real life SUPERHERO

> **Thought for the Day:**
> Sometimes it's braver to be Clark Kent than it is
> Superman. *Maybe?*

Brace yourself for a let-down.

We're sorry, but comic books and movies have misled you.

Not all superheroes wear capes. And that *'underpants on the outside'* thing? Not only is it odd and impractical, in the fashion stakes it's just plain wrong.

Here's the thing. You'll have *genuine* superheroes in your life, but you might not have noticed. They're in disguise, you see. Sure, your actual superheroes might sometimes wear tight-fitting Lycra, for the gym or yoga, but they are more likely to slob around the house in jeans and tee-shirt, undergarments firmly where they belong – on the *inside*.

And while the movies might have you believe in a lasso of truth, X-ray vision, or the ability to jump tall buildings, in their home environment superheroes are much more likely to wield the power of invisibility. Which is why you hardly notice them. They're first to rise in the morning, stealth-like. Ninjas of invisibility, they're showered, dressed, and ready to help get *everyone else* ready for the day ahead. Other family members won't notice that breakfast's ready, the fridge is stocked, the table is laid, the cups of tea are brewed, packed lunches packed . . .

Your typical everyday superheroes spend a lot of time washing up and/or loading and unloading the dishwasher.

Invisibly!

Unlike the movies, there's no brandishing of a 'spear of destiny' or 'shield of truth'. Instead, your real-life superhero is likely to be wielding a vacuum cleaner, have one hand in an oven glove, or both hands on an ironing board.

Real-life superheroes have the power to read minds. They know what you want for tea when sometimes you didn't even know you wanted it! They know where you left your coat, keys, shoes, etc. If you're little, they know you've got PE and that you'll need reminding to pack your kit (which will have been washed and folded in a two-day turnaround time using the superhero's power of speed).

Their powers of empathy are truly *extra*ordinary. Even when you've put on your bravest face and told them everything's fine, they somehow know that, really, everything's *not* fine. And then they stop time. In a world of whirring 'busyness' they stop everything for a seven-second hug, a magical moment when time stands still and the power of love is magically transferred. And in that gap where time has stopped, everything actually *is* okay. In fact, much better than okay. That hug has restorative powers.

But your real-life superhero's power of healing extends way beyond an *'I love you'* hug. One kiss of a grazed knee, one rub of a sore ankle, one wet flannel on a fevered forehead . . . and the wounded are walking again.

Real-life superheroes have the power of presence. In fact, the simple act of 'being there' is their most under-estimated super-power. As if by magic, superheroes appear when you need them most, and stick around for as long as necessary, curing you through their powers of listening.

The power of presence means they have an unerring reputation for showing up on the sidelines at their kids' rugby/football/hockey/chess/tennis/quidditch matches. They spend hours, standing in the rain, bigging the young ones up; win, lose, or draw. Superheroes sit through the two-hour school play, fidget-ing, but not grumbling, because they know their child will be searching for their face in the crowd. And when their eyes meet, there's a smile and small nod of encouragement, their 'can-do' power working its psychological magic.

It's the same in the workplace. Everyday superheroes can be seen wearing all sorts of outfits. Some wear a headset, a hard hat, tabard, overalls, or a tool belt. Superheroes often dress up as teachers, nurses, cleaners, firefighters, and plumbers. Superheroes sometimes work from home, hitting ridiculous deadlines and creating magical experiences for their customers. The job of some superheroes is to look after family members; old, young, often both.

Transport-wise, while a Batmobile might be ultra-cool, it's more likely your actual everyday superhero will drive a van, a lorry, or turn up at work in an ordinary car. Some travel on the bus, I've seen some on the Tube and, incredibly, some superheroes actually cycle to work!

But most of all, the superheroes in your life – the real ones, with underpants on the *inside* – have the power of super strength. They don't lift cars or buildings, they're much stronger than that.

They lift *you*.

Yes, somehow, they manage to support your weight, and theirs. They keep going, often against the odds.

They're there for you when you need them, even in the middle of the night.

Especially in the middle of the night.

Your real-life superheroes battle on, even when they're aching with exhaustion. They are the rock when the family seas are choppy. They make ends meet when the money's run out. They create an extra meal when a friend pops round. They conjure a magical day from an ordinary event; a picnic, a walk, a rainy day . . . somehow, and you're never quite sure how, these become the best days of your life.

And, here's a little known secret: superheroes can sometimes be kids! *Trainee* superheroes, I guess? You'll spot them doing their homework without being nagged, and doing it superbly. They're polite and hard working. You know the sort. They make you go 'wow'. It's a strange phenomenon, but superheroes tend to *produce* superheroes.

I suspect there's superhero DNA?

So, that said, here are four superhero lessons.

Superhero lesson #1: Just because those around you look normal, doesn't mean there's not a superhero inside, itching to get out. Ordinary everyday superheroes don't seek to be in the movies or in the comic books. They don't crave the limelight. They don't want you shouting it from the rooftops, but just occasionally, they might like a shout-out.

Superhero lesson #2: *So tell them!* When you spot one, catch them being amazing and call it out. Tell them how they've made you feel. Tell them what a difference they've made. Thank them for being kind, nice, helpful, or for simply being there for you. Tell them you love them.

Superhero lesson #3 is more sophisticated. Remember the first Harry Potter movie in which our speccy hero was living in cramped conditions underneath the stairs? He had no idea that he was a wizard! Indeed, it took a while for him to start believing in himself. Getting your Harry Potters, Diana Princes, and Peter Parkers to reveal themselves to the world is not always as easy as it seems. Remember, your superhero might not actually know they're a superhero. Sure they have powers, but their collective superhero kryptonite is their memories. Such *terrible* memories! Often, superheroes are so busy saving other people, that they simply forget how amazing they actually are.

So points 1 (noticing) and 2 (thanking) need to be done regularly, leading to superhero point #3. Here's another little-known superhero fact – their powers are replenished by one thing, and one thing only – it's called the *'hug of appreciation'*. If you want your superhero to stay in superhero mode, the hug of appreciation needs administering *daily*.

Yes, *DAILY!*

Which leads us on to our final superhero point . . .

Everyone's a superhero, including you. You're our hero and we reckon it's about time you started being yours.

So, let point #4 hit home:

You're a superhero. Stop pretending to be normal.

Rule #17

WORK IS FOR SCHMUCKS

Where are all
the watermelons?

> Definition:
> A karaoke life: *when you feel your life is to sing along to a song sheet written by somebody else. Moreover, there's a knot in your stomach as you realize there's no chance of ever getting the chance to write your own song.*

Work is called 'work' for a reason. Blue collar, white collar, it's all about labour. Often *hard* labour. 'Work' is a psychological contract in which you rent out a big chunk of your life to the highest bidder and, in return, they pay you some money so you can put food on the table. The harder you work, the more you can afford. Bottom line, you work because you need the money. You'd prefer *not* to have to work. Everyone looks forward to days off, weekends, holidays . . . retirement. Right?

Wrong!

Not quite 'everyone'. There are a few who don't 'labour'. At least not in the traditional sense of the word. They love what they do. For this small minority, work isn't 'work' at all. It's a joy and pleasure. Sure, these people get paid but that's a bonus. They're not turning up for the money. In fact, whisper it very quietly, but they'd probably do it for free.

So the billion-dollar question is, how on earth do I become one of the non-workers? How can I craft a life where work doesn't feel like work?

It just so happens that Pouli's arrived at that place, but via a circuitous route. His journey is a lesson to us all.

'Don't eat the seeds or you'll grow a watermelon in your belly.'
That's the warning my parents would always give my younger
brother and I when we were little kids enjoying some watermelon
in our backyard. To avoid eating those pesky watermelon seeds
we'd either spit them out or pick them out with our fingers. Have
you ever tried to handle a watermelon seed? They are so slippery!
If you squeeze them between your fingers, you can shoot them
off into some random direction at a pretty high speed.

They can travel real far. I know, because my bro and I had compe-
titions. Summer after glorious summer we ate watermelon and
littered the backyard with watermelon seeds. Until one day it
occurred to me that with all these watermelon seeds in our
backyard, it should be covered with watermelons.

And yet it wasn't. As a matter of fact, I don't recall a single
watermelon growing in our backyard during my entire childhood.
Which got me wondering about a question we're going to come
back to later: *where are all the watermelons?*

When I wasn't sitting in the backyard eating watermelon, you
would find me with my head in a science fiction novel or glued
in front of Star Trek re-runs. I built spaceships and strange
machines using balsa wood, electronic components, and
hacked-together parts from multiple model kits. My sci-fi
geekiness also extended into story writing and art. My bedroom
was plastered with my drawings of aliens, starships, and robots.
In my mind, there was a story behind every drawing and scratch-
built model.

The adults in my life told me that 'art' and 'stories' were wonderful hobbies that I could keep going in the background. Meantime,

I needed to work towards a proper job – a *career* – something safe and solid.

The most obvious and sensible option for a young man who builds spaceships in his spare time is to enrol on a degree in electrical engineering, so fast forward to my late teenage years and that certainty became nailed on. Indeed, it was a perfectly fine degree at a perfectly fine university, with the exception of one stand-out semester that rose way above 'fine'. It just so happened that in college I had the opportunity to teach physics at a local high school as part of a learning project for budding engineering students. I loved every minute of teaching that semester-long course. And I mean every minute: prepping, inventing fun and engaging stories to make the physics concepts clear to my students, and especially the teaching bit. On reflection, I taught them by stealth. My style was to entertain the students and once fully engaged I'd sneak in the hard-core science lessons without them really noticing.

Anyhow, that semester zipped by and I returned to the mundane, completed my degree, and was hired into a prestigious multinational technology company. From the outside looking in, it looked like I'd landed on my feet. It was a good job – a *proper* job – in fact it was a *career*, with a nice salary and pension. But from the inside looking out I was a backyard watermelon seed. I'd landed in the wrong environment.

I watched many of my peers land in the same career and germinate immediately. They sprouted, grew, and flourished in engineering soil. What was wrong with me? Why was I wilting? Maybe I needed to work harder? Yes, that was it. If I got even better qualified then engineering might click for me, so that's exactly what I did. I knuckled down and worked even harder at my uninspiring career, completing my master's degree, hoping that my motivation would magically fall into place.

And guess what? It didn't.

With great hindsight of 30 years in the rear-view mirror, I realize the flow state I felt while teaching physics in that high school classroom was a result of the joy of striving towards my truest potential. That was my calling. In fact my calling had been screaming at me for three decades, but I hadn't been listening! Suffice to say that after a number of career challenges, hurdles, and restarts, I am a professional speaker, trainer, consultant, and a senior lecturer at a business university in America. It's a dream job that allows me to focus on the work I enjoy doing well. And guess what? I aim to entertain my students and once I've lulled them in through stories, I hit them with the hard-core marketing and sales syllabus without them really noticing.

And because I like being good at the work of teaching, I am constantly striving to get better at the craft.

I'm hoping that there's a lesson in my 30-year journey. Maybe it's a lesson about daring to walk the unexpected path. Or maybe it's a lesson about not ignoring the clues. Or when your calling's calling, listen and act. It might even be 'it's never too late to give up', with this particular watermelon seed still being able to germinate after 30 years!

In my case, I fell into engineering because of love. I didn't love engineering but the people closest to me, those who loved me and had my very best intentions at heart, *accidentally* smoothed the way to a career that I didn't want.

On the surface, *'You're great at math, and science, and building things so you should be an engineer'* seems like natural and sensible advice. But the big leap of faith is to assume that just because we're skilled at the tasks, we will enjoy the work.

Admittedly, it does sometimes work like that, but not in my case. And evidence stacks up elsewhere. We've been encouraging people to follow career paths based on their strengths and natural abilities for as long as we've been sending people off to work. And, guess what, 70% of people in the workforce today are dissatisfied and disengaged from their jobs.

What are we missing?

The question we've been asking is too simple. We typically ask: *what do you do well?*

When we actually need to upgrade to a two-parter: *what do you do well **and** enjoy doing?*

It's never guaranteed that what you do well is something you enjoy doing.

But when it comes time to figure out what you do well and enjoy doing, people often get stuck. I developed the Career Satisfaction Matrix™ to unstick my students (see Figure 17.1). The matrix has two axes: Skill Level and Enjoyment Level.

Here's how you use the Career Satisfaction Matrix™. Begin by answering the following questions:

1. Think back over the last week, month, or year and just make a long list of the tasks you do in your current role.

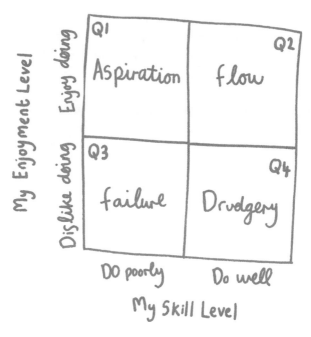

Figure 17.1 The Career Satisfaction Matrix.

2. Once you've made your list, estimate the percentage of time you spend doing each type of task.
3. Go through each task on your list and decide if you **do it well** or **do it poorly**. (For this exercise, define 'doing it poorly' as below average performance.)
4. Once you've divided the list into 'do well' and 'do poorly', go through the list again and decide if you **enjoy doing** or **dislike doing** this type of task.

You can transfer each item from this list of tasks onto the matrix to help you visualize where you spend the majority of your time throughout a typical work week or work year. Each task will fit into one of the following four quadrants:

ASPIRATION: tasks you enjoy but could do with learning to do better

The prescription for you in this quadrant is to focus on mastery. Take some courses, find mentors, get some training, and learn how to do those tasks better. Try to spend more time doing that type of work to advance your skills. Learning how to improve on skills you enjoy using will not feel like 'work'.

FAILURE: tasks you dislike doing and do poorly

You will find it difficult to improve your job performance because you don't enjoy the task and you have no real natural skills for doing the work. You will likely fail in this role. This is the danger zone. It's past time to find another career path.

DRUDGERY: tasks you're rather good at, but don't enjoy doing

The issue with this quadrant is that people are likely to push more of these tasks your way, because you do them well. The result is that more and more boredom sets in. It'll feel tedious and you need to find a way to minimize the amount of time you spend doing that task. That might mean changing jobs. That might mean discussing the situation with your manager and deciding to shift some of the responsibility to someone else who perhaps enjoys doing that kind of work, or maybe allows you to train someone to take over that part of the job from you.

FLOW: tasks you enjoy doing and do well

When you do something well and enjoy doing it, you will often find yourself in a psychological state of 'flow'. You'll be fully immersed in whatever it is you're doing. You feel energized, you enjoy the process of doing the work, and it may feel like time ceases to exist. Try to spend as much time as possible in these types of tasks because this is the sweet spot where work doesn't feel like work.

There is a danger lurking in this Nirvana-like quadrant: the better you perform these types of tasks, the more likely you will be asked to take on more responsibility. For example, if you are an excellent salesperson, you may be asked to take a promotion and become a Director of Sales where you manage people. The promotion may be a 'reward' for your outstanding work as an individual contributor, but you may be moving into a role which might put you into a position of doing things you do not enjoy (managing people, forecasting revenue, training employees). If you're not mindful of what you enjoy doing well, you can find yourself in another quadrant which may be difficult to escape once the promotion has been put in place.

Very few people get to do their dream job all day every day. There will be elements of your work that fall into all four quadrants. We're merely bringing something fairly obvious to your attention – too long in the Drudgery and/or Failure quadrants will do you no good whatsoever. It'll be difficult to stay motivated and work will feel very much like hard labour. And this matters greatly if you want to become one of the non-workers – the minority who *don't* get that 'minor glumness' feeling on Monday morning.

Indeed, there's evidence that glumness is coming earlier. The mid-life crisis has migrated to the under 30s in what's known as a quarter-life crisis. Yes, the sense of *'is this it?'* is kicking in three decades earlier. By 25, life has hit you squarely in the face. That dream job is a dream alright – a proper 70-hour-a-week nightmare that keeps you awake with worry. That wonderful salary just about covers your stupefying monthly rent. Your commute is hardly a joyride. As for partying, hah! Your spare time is spent catching up on sleep.

We spend a lifetime getting ready for our careers. We plan for the perfect entry into the workplace and then – poof – virtually everyone is unhappy, unsatisfied, unmotivated, and disengaged.

How did this happen? How did we *let* it happen?

Where are all the flourishing people?

Where are all the watermelons?

Back to my earlier point. Watermelon seeds that are squeezed between your fingers will shoot out at high speed and in random directions. They have a pretty impressive flight with an abrupt landing. However, they invariably land someplace that is not conducive to growth. They may end up sitting on top of grass where birds snatch them up or on asphalt where they dry out in the heat of the sun.

They don't have the chance to germinate in an environment that is conducive to their growth. They receive too little water and dry out or they receive too much water and drown.

But you can learn to take control of your watermelon seed's path.

For decades now, young people have spent less time discovering their passions, their natural abilities, and their core strengths. They spend less time doing tasks and activities purely for internally motivated enjoyment. Besides the rise in job dissatisfaction, the real tragedy is the rise in issues related to anxiety and depression. In the last 50 years, the number of children and college students reporting clinically significant depression or anxiety has increased by 700%. In the last 50 years, suicide rates have doubled for the 15 to 25 age bracket and quadrupled for the under 15s.

Just like seeds, your dreams and goals need to be protected from dream killers, the people and the circumstances that accidentally sap your energy and willpower. Find the people who share your passions and interests. Spend time with them and they will protect and amplify your dreams.

Moving from Aspiration to Flow is a journey of great personal growth. You will feel challenged as you improve your skills in areas of work you enjoy doing. As you approach Flow, higher levels of performance will feel easier. You'll look forward to each work day and you'll embrace multiple opportunities for learning new skills. You will be in a perpetual state of seeking greater mastery which is great for you, your work colleagues, and your customers.

Best of all, you have become one of the non-workers because work doesn't feel like 'work'.

Rule #18

ACT YOUR SHOE SIZE

"If anyone asks i'm four and a half years old"

> *A good question?*
> *I want to reach your mind. Where is it currently located?*

There's an adage that suggests you should act your age, not your shoe size. It's usually said by someone having a dig at you for being a bit childlike.

But one of the secrets of truly living is to actually be more like a child. Hence you might be better off reverse engineering their advice. Sometimes, acting your shoe size might get you a better result.

Here's a true story to make our point:

Dr Andy did an event at a school in the north of England. Here's his school report and, as is the way with schools, there are always lessons to be learned. Brace yourself for six of the best . . .

I was delivering a wellbeing programme to an amazing audience of 65 ten-year-olds. It was a fabulous two days.

Day one: it was going extraordinarily well. The staff and kids were a joy. At 10.30, as it does every day, a bell heralded morning break. The kids did what the kids always do at playtime. The clue's in the name.

They went outside to *play*.

And, of course, I did what was expected of the adults – I followed them along a corridor to the staffroom where I stood, dipped a custard cream into my instant coffee, and made small talk.

I listened in on the children's background stories. I learned that things went missing when Connor was around, that Phoebe had anxiety and already, at age 10, Chloe had issues with food.

While I listened, I looked out of the staffroom window, marvelling as 250 children buzzed around the playground in a swarm of excitement, energy, and unbridled glee. It was a beautifully animated scene – a whirlwind of tag, hopscotch, skipping, WWF wrestling, and imaginary games. The soundtrack was one of high-pitched screaming, shouting, and squeals.

My gaze was drawn to two little girls playing amongst the throng. One was twirling around while her BFF guided her across the length of the tarmac, their game seemingly to count *'how many twirls does it take to get across the playground?'*

I was mesmerized not only by the sublime simplicity of their game, but by their total immersion. I watched as they twirled through a game of football, oblivious to it, the boys actually stopping and watching, before continuing the rough stuff after the little girls had twirled safely through.

Alas, before they'd finished twirling, someone rang a big brass bell and the scene became *suspended* animation. As if by magic, 250 dervishes were frozen in whatever moment they were in. One of the footballers had just scored a goal and was in mid-celebration, suspended in the moment with arms aloft, eyes wide, mouth even wider, his face etched with glee.

I remember thinking, if the world ends now, it ends well for him.

   [Lesson #1: That's how I want to go.]

A few seconds later there came a second ringing of the bell, which seemingly released the children from their suspended animation and they did what they do every breaktime – they lined up to go back into school.

I watched the whole 'frozen/unfrozen, get-lined-up' thing unfold. Everyone knows the rules because the same thing happens every day. The whole choreography takes 45 seconds. The aim is to restore order. Once the bees have stopped buzzing, they file quietly and regimentally back into school.

I noticed that the bell also signalled the teachers to do what teachers do when they hear a bell. Pavlov-style, they slurp the last dregs, stick their dirty cup in the sink, and hurry back to class.

I was the last to leave the staffroom. I wandered back to my class, deep in thought.

That's when I was struck by an intriguing inspiration.

My crowd of 65 settled back into their places. 'Gosh kids', I said, 'I've just watched you playing outside. Sooooo much energy!' Feeling a little devilish, I said, 'So how about tomorrow we do a world first. Something that's never been attempted ever before . . .'

The kids were sitting up, interested.

'Tomorrow, at morning break, how about we switch things around. What if me and you lot go to the staffroom and we send the staff out for *playtime!*'

There was a moment of absolutely nothing but furrowed brows, broken by Phoebe's hesitantly anxious question, 'I don't think you're allowed to do that?'

'Exactly Phoeb-ster!' I beamed. 'Let's make it happen.'

[Lesson #2: Always consult the head teacher before you make rash decisions or promises.]

The head teacher wasn't keen but I managed to twist her arm and against her better judgement, next day, it was game on!

My 65 kids arrived at school, *early*. Yes, all of them, bright-eyed and eager, queuing at the school gates waiting to be let in. For context – kids arriving at school *before* the caretaker opens up, that had never happened in the history of the school.

Or, indeed, any school. *Ever!*

I high-fived them into class. They were proper pumped, not just for the wellbeing lessons, but for being allowed to take over the staffroom at breaktime. 'Is it happening?' asked Connor, trying to sound matter-of-fact (but in actual fact planning a heist).

I nodded. The kids cheered. There was almost no learning that morning because I had my hands full just keeping the lid on their excitement.

[Lesson #3: You can be too excited!]

The bell sounded. *Breaktime!* I led 65 excited children down the corridor to the staffroom, while 37 adults went outside for playtime. For the record, every single adult in the entire school had gone out for playtime. It was me, and 65 ten-year olds, with a kettle!

The atmosphere was something I'd never experienced before. There were 64 kids messing around with tea bags and boiling water, while the 65th (Connor) was taking full advantage of the chaos by rifling through the teachers' handbags, executing his heist to perfection.

Harry had found the teachers' secret stash of chocolates and was sharing them around, with everyone tucking in except Chloe (*I don't wanna get fat*) and Phoebe (*I'm not sure we're allowed?*)

The kids were already giddy from being in the staffroom but the combo of caffeine and sugar had elevated 'giddy' to 'giddy heights'.

Truth told, it was utter chaos. I was out of my depth. I needed a distraction so, over-acting terribly, I pointed to the staffroom window and shouted, 'Oh my goodness! Look out there. Have you ever seen anything so amazing?'

The kids downed their kettles, cups, chocolates (and Connor his wallets and purses) and rushed to the window, 65 noses pressed against the pane, 65 pairs of eyes resting on 37 adults, stood awkwardly in the playground. There was no laughter, no running, no tag, no stuck-in-the-mud, no teachers in a WWF clinch, and absolutely no *'how many twirls does it take to get across the playground?'*

The grown-ups just stood there, not quite knowing what to do.

For the whole 20 minutes!

The children wore genuine looks of perplexity. Phoebe's anxiety was flaring up. She pointed at the adults and looked at me expectantly. 'Andy, why aren't they playing?' she asked.

I shrugged. 'Phoebes, I'm not entirely sure, but I think they might have just forgotten how.'

[Lesson #4: What if the previous sentence is about as close to the truth as you will ever get?]

[Lesson #5: What if happiness isn't about a whole load of new tips, tricks, and techniques. What if the real 'secret' of happiness lies in getting back to how we used to be. What if happiness is about reconnecting with our inner child, or simply being more playful, more often?]

[Lesson #6: My shoe size is 8½. Yep, that sounds about right.]

CARRY
ON *SQUEEZING*

Be A Squeezer!

Tweetable #ThoughtfortheDay:

You don't get what you wish for; you get what you *work* for

Take yourself to your bathroom for a slightly dated analogy.

I know . . . just go with it.

The bathroom may well be the only place you spend time by yourself without technology (unless you're a toilet texter in which case I beat my chest in anguish, claw at my skin, and howl at the sky . . . *WHYYYYYYY?*).

The bathroom provides sanctuary. Me time. At the very least there's a toilet, somewhere to wash, and a mirror. You do stuff in the bathroom that's private. Stuff you really wouldn't want other people to see. That mirror will have seen some sights:

You toileting and, if you're male, missing!

You puking up in the toilet bowl.

You first thing on a Monday morning.

You after a night out.

You after sex.

You before sex.

~~You having…~~

You practising your smile.

You squeezing your zits.

You looking and wondering, pinching an inch, checking the wrinkles, clearing the sleep from your eyes, checking your boobs/moobs.

You at your sparkly dressed-up best, puckering up to the mirror and blowing yourself a kiss before a big night out.

Maybe even you saying positive affirmations that you don't quite believe; *'I'm a tiger, I'm a tiger, I'M A TIGER'*.

But mostly, day in day out, you'll have watched yourself brush your teeth.

The toothbrush will have changed over the years, as well as the type of toothpaste (sensitive, whitening, healthy gums, fresh breath, extra minty, repair and protect, ultra clean, or good old original . . .), but the basic chore of cleaning your pearly whites has stayed the same.

So, because it's such a basic thing, let's spend some time with the toothpaste tube.

If you're lucky enough to get a fresh tube, the first squeeze is the best. *Easy-peasy toothpaste squeezy*. The tube is generous. One tiny squeeze fills your brush.

A few days later you have to squeeze slightly more to get the same amount of toothpaste. You might be getting miffed at those in your family who are middle squeezers.

A few days more and it's a struggle. A big *squeeeeeeze* spits out very little. That particular tube of toothpaste is on its last legs.

So here's the killer question: *are you a toothpaste tube roller-upper?*

Or, when the going gets tough, do you bin it and start afresh, with a brand new big fat sausage-shaped easy-peasy squeezer?

Because – breaking news folks – this is where the magic happens. The moment when you think you cannot possibly get any more from the tube is when you will always find extra.

So here's a new word for you; *sisu*. It's a Finnish word for the toothpaste *squeeeeeze*. Sisu relates to the psychological strength that allows a person to overcome extraordinary challenges. Sisu is similar to what we might call perseverance, or the trendier concept of grit. When you're running on empty and you're not sure you can carry on, sisu is your emergency 'reserve tank' that somehow keeps you going.

Whatever you call it – sisu, grit, bravery, resilience, bothered-ness . . . it all points to developing a backbone instead of a wishbone.

And that extra *squeeeeeze*, over time, makes a massive difference.

It's why the last 20% of a workout is horrifying, but the feeling on the other side is WOW. The extra effort required for prepping a meal is time-consuming, but once you've plated it and taken that first mouthful, the effort is forgotten. The hours of studying for an exam are a nightmare but when you smash it, you can bask in a job well done.

These wow moments can only ever arise from your bothered-ness. You have to keep squeezing even when it looks like there's nothing left to be had. We're not saying it's easy (because if it was then everyone would do it), but we're promising it's worth it.

In the long run, that is.

Because botheredness moves you streets ahead of the non-squeezers; the masses who talk a good talk but end up with the other runners and riders, the non-squeezers.

Too many folk will start a new diet, workout plan, relationship, job, business idea, adventure . . . and give up at the first sign of difficulty.

We've re-written Angela Duckworth's botheredness formula (she calls it 'grit', but hey, it's the same thing), in which the *squeeeeeze* counts twice:

First up, *talent x squeeeeeze = skill*

When you consider individuals in identical circumstances, what each achieves depends on just two things, talent and effort. Talent relates to how fast we can improve in skill. Applying it to a subject, say tennis, a little bit of talent is useful, but talent without effort means you'll never get skilful.

But also, *skill x squeeeeeze = achievement*

Once you've got skillful, it is effort that makes the breakthrough to achievement.

Actor Will Smith articulates it well by admitting that he never really considered himself talented; *'. . . where I excel is ridiculous, sickening work ethic'.* He goes on, *'I will not be outworked. You might have more talent than me, be smarter than me, you might be sexier than me. You might be all of those things. You got me in nine categories. But if we get on the treadmill together, there's two things. You're getting off first, or I'm gonna die. It's really that simple.'*

Will's clearly a *squeeeeeezer!*

Deciding to do something is common. Indeed, enthusiasm is common. But endurance is rare, because it takes effort to keep going.

It's a whole lot easier to stop. *And that's the problem*.

The end result is that most people live well within their limits. There seems little point in being energized below your maximum and behaving below your optimum. It's like driving a Lamborghini at 27mph. Or worse, it's like being in possession of a whole load of superpowers that you fail to use. I mean, who would you rather be, Peter Parker or Spidey; Diana Prince or Wonder Woman?

More darn truth!

'We all love to win, but how many people love training?'

Mark Spitz: Multi-gold Olympic swimmer and squeeeeeezer

Try this: write down a list of people you admire. People who've achieved things. Your heroes.

1. _____
2. _____
3. _____

4. _____

5. _____

We're pretty sure your list will consist of talented people – actors, pop stars, sporting legends – that kind of thing. The modern world promotes the cult of genius. We are conned into thinking genius is something magical. It's a huge get-out clause which tells us that we're not obliged to compare ourselves with geniuses because they were born that way.

But were they?

Were they *really?*

Or was there some serious effort and botheredness involved?

Your heroes, they're *squeeeeezers*.

So squeeeeeze life. *And keep on squeeeeeeeeeeezing!*

Rule #20

BEING BUSY AND BEING PRODUCTIVE ARE TWO DIFFERENT THINGS

3x water buckets

ɤ an almost true story...

> Fact:
> *A smooth sea never made a skilful mariner*

[Almost] True story:

Syd had risen through the ranks, from intern to department manager in double quick time. He considered himself to be an excellent boss – a listener – who took great pride in how efficiently he managed his department. Syd had been on many management courses. He loved the words 'initiative', 'empowerment', 'coaching', and his absolute favourite was 'proactive'.

Syd's team worked in an office with a flat roof and one day during some heavy rain one of his staff, Sandra, brought to his attention that the roof was leaking and water was dripping into the office.

Syd instinctively knew the answer but, ever the coach, he bit his tongue. Instead, Syd asked his favourite coaching question; *'Sandra'*, he smiled, *'what do you think we should do about the dripping water?'*

Two minutes later Sandra had implemented her idea (which also happened to be Syd's idea, the one he'd had *before* biting his tongue) and Syd went back to his emails with one eye on the office situation. He nodded in satisfaction as his employee found a metal wastepaper basket and placed it under the drip. And, gosh, he was super-impressed that she padded the bin with paper towels, so the *drip drip drip* sound was absorbed.

Syd was very pleased. He hadn't even asked her to do the paper towel thing. He considered it initiative extraordinaire. Not only was the problem resolved, but he'd also empowered Sandra.

About an hour later, Sandra popped her head into the office to report that the bucket was nearly full. She reminded Syd that if it spilled there'd be a wet floor which meant a potential health and safety incident.

A health and safety incident? This time Syd didn't need any words. He looked up from his emails and did his eyebrow thing, and sure enough Sandra just knew. It had been drummed into them that health and safety was THE ABSOLUTE PRIORITY. She found a bucket from the caretaker's room and placed that under the drip, emptied the first and placed it alongside, ready to be filled again.

Now a simple system was in place.

Syd cracked on with his emails, delighted with Sandra's initiative, relieved that the health and safety incident had been averted, but his mind whirring.

There was an office junior, on lower pay than Sandra. Would it not make sense for Ravi to take responsibility for the bucket emptying? This would surely be a case of job enrichment, added responsibility, and employee development. So during the next storm, he called Ravi into the office, explained the problem, explained about wet floors and health and safety, and coached the young man in the entire bucket-emptying system. The leak was getting worse so they agreed to add a third bucket to the system, just in case. Then, as a good coach does, Syd handed over the responsibility to Ravi, giving himself and Sandra a free run at their backlog of emails.

Genius!

Syd was careful to monitor Ravi's performance on a regular basis. Alas, as often happens in these situations, Ravi soon left the organization. Syd had a meeting with Sandra and they agreed this was a golden opportunity to include responsibility for 'bucket emptying' in the job description. So when Martha started work in Ravi's old job, she took on the additional responsibility, with paper-towel training of course.

The office hummed with efficiency and even when the rain hammered down, the bucket system kept the floors dry. The final piece in the bucket-emptying jigsaw came quite by accident and from the most unlikely of sources. Jake, the IT guy, who hardly ever speaks up in meetings, actually suggested he could create a sensor which could be placed on the roof of the office to tell the computer when it was raining. The computer would then send a message to Martha's desk, reminding her to empty the bucket.

Perfect! The potential health and safety incident had been permanently averted.

Syd was proud to be in charge of such a proactive team and, of course, his leadership style didn't go un-noticed. A couple of months later there was cake and pressies and Syd was off, promoted to head office, to work his leadership magic on a much larger scale.

Sandra got his job and is currently working with Jake and the IT team on the design of an automated bucket emptying device.

Meanwhile Brenda, who cleans the office, keeps asking *'Why doesn't someone mend the f***ing roof!'*

***

We hope you enjoyed our modern parable. We changed the names and the scenario, but the point is bang on.

Being busy and being productive are two different things.

The solutions lie elsewhere in this book, so we thought we'd throw half a dozen questions your way instead:

1. How many 'leaking roofs' are there in your organization?
2. How many leaking roofs are there in your *life*?
3. How often do we over-complicate things, at work and home?
4. It's perfectly okay to be super-busy. But how often are you super-busy *doing the wrong things?*
5. What would happen if you stripped away all the bullshit and got busy doing the things that *really* matter?
6. And, talking of which, what are those things? If, say, there were five things that really mattered in your life, what would those five be?

The menial will get in the way of the meaningful if you let it.

SO DON'T!

Rule #21

YOU ARE MADE OF ORDINARY MAGIC

IMPORTANT NOTE:

You must take care of yourself in life before you can take care of anyone else.

> *'Those who don't believe in magic will never find it.'*
> – Roald Dahl

All 7.5 billion people on this planet are miracles.

But one of your three authors is more miraculous than most.

Whenever Pouli has an appointment with a healthcare professional that he's never visited before, he brings a printed copy of his surgical history, a sheaf of papers which regales the gory details of the 20 surgeries he's had over the last three decades.

Yes folks, that equates to one major scalpel incision every 1.5 years of his adult life.

Medical records are private, but Pouli is happy to reveal that his list begins in 1982 with *arthroscopic surgery to repair torn right knee cartilage* and, at time of writing, ends with *surgery to repair a torn retina*.

In between those dates there are two total knee replacement surgeries, five (yes 5!) hip replacements, two torn bicep tendon repairs, a vasectomy, and a vasectomy reversal. For those old enough to remember Lee Majors, Pouli is the Six Million Dollar Man. Those airport metal detectors start buzzing as soon as he pulls up in the taxi!

You wouldn't have to go very far back in modern history to arrive at a point where Pouli would be wheelchair bound, housebound, or dead. And yet, thanks to modern health care, he remains very much alive. In fact, Pouli is planning to climb Kilimanjaro so I'd say he's more than 'alive', he's 'truly living'.

But of course, if the list was expanded to include other life challenges Pouli's faced along the way, there would be two occurrences of being laid off from a multinational company, one incident of being fired from a senior role at a small start-up, several nearest and dearest's funerals attended, and one battle with depression.

This sounds pretty grim, but if you look back over your own life and catalogue the hardships you've faced – and *survived* – you will likely have a similar list. Life is indeed a contact sport. It's safe to assume that nobody else has had a free pass or easy life.

Our point?

Physically, you're going to accumulate knocks, breakages, bruises, scratches, and dents. If Pouli rolls up his trouser leg and shows you his knees, the scars are there for all to see.

But we are also buffeted psychologically. Yet with emotional trauma, it's not merely a case of the medical profession slicing you open and removing the offending part. Mental ill-health can be much more debilitating and significantly longer lasting. And, crucially, the internal nature of emotional damage means there is nothing to see.

Which is why I was surprised when Pouli mentioned his depression to me. He's so bouncy!

Depression crept up on Pouli while languishing in the Drudgery Zone (see rule #17), working in a job that was a bad fit for him.

Pouli explains that it was a whole lot easier to get back on his feet after five hip replacements than a bout of depression.

The thing about Pouli is that he has positive DNA. Even during his darkest periods, he was able to mask his inner pain with a brave face. So nobody knew, except those closest to him. As is often the case with depression, your nearest and dearest cannot be fooled. Pouli's depression was devastating for him personally, and for his wife and kids.

For Pouli, there's a happy ending. He got the help he needed, he changed his circumstances, his depression dissipated and has not resurfaced for over 10 years.

The thing is, Pouli's depressive episode is not unusual. The stats are common knowledge so we're not going to trot them out, other than to point out that they're going the *wrong* way. There's something about the modern world that has caused mental ill-health to rise exponentially.

To unearth something very powerful, let's park the modern world and go back in time, to *olde worlde* Japan of 500 years ago. If you've ever wandered through an art museum and come across ancient, broken pots that have been glued back together, you may have been exposed to *kintsugi*, something that roughly translates as 'golden seams' or 'golden joinery'.

Imagine that a pot has fallen on the floor and smashed. In kintsugi, the pieces are lovingly pieced back together with gold infused glue, the end result being that every single crack is deliberately highlighted. Google 'kintsugi'. It's quite something.

The wonder of kintsugi is this . . . the broken pot is deemed more beautiful *after* it's been pieced back together. The breakages have not ruined the pot or destroyed its aesthetics. On the contrary, kintsugi deems that the pot is enhanced when all its flaws are deliberately exposed.

And we can't help thinking there's something in there about people.

Pouli's physical and mental history suggests that we're all human kintsugi. We're all broken. But the scars, the damage, the breakages, the flaws: these ARE part of the beauty.

We're not saying you should go around bragging about your imperfections, merely that your breakages have made you who you are. You are *you* because of them.

Sci-fi Kintsugi

'Damn it, Bones, you're a doctor. You know pain and guilt can't be taken away with a wave of a magic wand. They're the things we carry with us, the things that make us who we are. If we lose them, we lose ourselves. I don't want my pain taken away. I need my pain.'

– James T. Kirk, Star Trek V: The Final Frontier

Pouli describes the one major epiphany that occurred to him during his battle with depression: *you must take care of yourself in life before you can take care of anyone else.* It's the often used metaphor of the flight attendant reminding us that, in the event of an emergency, we need to put our own oxygen masks on first before trying to help someone else get their mask on. It might be a rather well-worn cliché, but in terms of mental WEALTH, it's absolutely true.

Here is Pouli's story:

In the years leading up to my depression, I prioritized everyone else's needs and desires over my own. I was in a career that did not reward me for using my natural abilities and skills. I never really saw the impact I was having on the company or the customers we served. Most of my co-workers were more interested in corporate politics than serving some inspiring purpose. I truly disliked, actually *despised*, the work, but I felt compelled to try and succeed in this type of corporate setting where so many of my peers seemed to thrive. I spent 30 years trying to figure it all out but it took an external force – lay off – to force me to hit rock bottom professionally, financially, and personally.

The best advice I received during this time was quite simple: you need to focus on your mental health completely. If circumstances get worse, you'll need to be strong and whole to survive. If things get better, you'll need to be whole in order to move forward and take advantage of whatever opportunities lie on the other side of the darkness.

By taking care of myself I became a better father, husband, friend, and co-worker. And it all led me to a career path that is a calling not a pay cheque. Nowadays, I see opportunity at every corner. My perspective has shifted 180 degrees, but nobody taught me how. I had to experience it in order to figure it out for myself.

Therapists call it 'post-traumatic growth'. Related to kintsugi, we are all more valuable to our loved ones *because* of the battles we've fought, regardless of whether we won or lost them. The key is in our ability to learn from all these battles and keep moving forward while proudly embracing our gold-filled scars.

All of us have fought through battles, whether they have been physical, mental, social, or spiritual. The key is not to dwell on the battle but to 'mine the gold' in understanding what we have gained from the experience of the battle.

Make a list of the top five 'battles' you can remember fighting in your life. Big or small, it doesn't matter, just get it into a list. For each item, answer the following questions:

1. What was my initial reaction to the situation?
2. What did I fear most as the adversity unfolded?
3. How did I fight this battle? What did I do to survive?
4. What did I learn about myself as a result?
5. How has my behaviour changed *for the better* after this adversity?
6. What would I have missed about myself had I not fought through?

We three think the human/kintsugi analogy is powerful stuff. In fact, it's a big chunk missing from the school curriculum.

At the age of 53 I'm beginning to doubt I'll ever need to create the algebraic formula that my maths teacher considered so vital. Instead, I wish he'd taught me how to hurt, and I mean *truly* hurt, to see my father or brother grieving in front of me.

And although school taught me poetry, it never taught me how to love. How to *truly* love, how to selflessly commit to someone else. *For life!*

And dissecting a frog was all well and good but I never learned about what's inside of me, how to be resilient or to make ends meet. I never learned how to get up each and every day, filled with dread for whatever lay ahead, and to keep going against the odds.

School never taught me how to sit by a hospital bed for days on end. How to console. How to empathize.

We dabbled in foreign languages but never with the voice in my own head; how to live with my demons, disappointments, and nagging self-doubt. They didn't teach me how to *truly* push back at life when it closes in on you.

And the biggest missing link is that nobody (not at school, college, or in life) ever teaches you how to love yourself, how to build mental strength that doesn't wax and wane when the world throws its worst your way.

Which it damn well will!

In short, we are human kintsugi. Yes, all of us. Even the ones who pretend they haven't got scars.

Two truths become crucial in understanding our kintsugi nature.

First, just because you have messed up doesn't mean you *are* messed up. Bad stuff will surely feel bad. But it's part of the journey. You're learning what it takes to be human.

What it takes to be *real*.

If you're to fall in love with life you have to embrace the *whole* show; the laughing, crying, terrifying, angry, happy, sad, joyous, embarrassing, boring, regrettable bits . . . this is our life.

Once the penny drops, you are unstoppable.

Second (and somewhat bizarrely), when you realize life is hard, it gets easier.

You possess what's called 'ordinary magic', otherwise known as 'time'. Remember what you are made of the next time you think you are bulletproof. You are flesh and bone and blood, with a heart made of glass. Stop trying to pretend you're indestructible – like any emotional creature it is in your nature to bend, like any emotional creature it is in your nature to break, and like any emotional creature it is in your nature to *heal*.

Healing doesn't just take time, it takes courage. It takes guts to pick yourself up from the wreckage, dust off your limbs, bandage your hurts, and move on. Kintsugi suggests that survival is more than burying the damage, it is about *befriending* it.

Moreover, it's about being *thankful* for it.

You are damaged goods. And you are YOU because of it.

Rule #22

QUIT YOUR 'WAIT PROBLEM'

wakey wakey
the time to be
HAPPY is...

> The best time to plant a tree was 20 years ago. The second best
> time is now.
>
> *Chinese proverb*

No modern-day personal development book is worth its salt
unless it finds time for a quick moment about moments. So here's
a 100% true tale that happened to Dr Andy.

It happened to be February and I'd just wrapped up the delivery
of my all-time favourite workshop 'The Art of Being Brilliant'. A
spring in their step, the delegates gradually dispersed and I set
about dismantling my laptop, projector, and speakers.

One delegate lingered, awkwardly. I was ever so keen to get
home for my tea, but the guy's uncomfortably close proximity
meant I had no choice but to acknowledge him.

'What struck me today', he frowned, 'was that you've not taught
me a single damn thing'.

I stopped mid-tidy, gulped, and fronted up. 'Gosh, sorry
about that.'

'Oh, it's not a criticism', smiled the man. 'It's been a brilliant day.
You've reminded me of a whole load of really important things
I've got to start doing. For me, it's not been about personal
development, it's been a day of personal remembering.'

I smiled. There was an inner *phew* and I continued coiling my
extension lead. Bag nearly packed, the lingerer re-lingered, this

time with a diary and pencil. 'I'm committed to action', he beamed. 'And I want you to be my witness.'

The man sat at a table and beckoned me to the adjacent chair.

'It's been a big fat reminder', said the lingerer. 'So I'm going to change. I'm going to be happier and more positive, at work and home. I'm committed to doing the things you said. All of them.'

'Excellent', I smiled.

'And I'm going to start doing them on November the first.'

I blinked hard. Remember, this was February.

The man licked his finger and started flicking through his paper diary. Right there in front of me he flicked out loud, 'February, March, April, May . . .' as he turned the pages. 'June, July, August, September, October . . .' He arrived at November 1st and pressed with a sharp pencil: 'START TO BE BRILLIANT TODAY!!!!!'

The man beamed at me, delighted at his commitment. 'There it is, etched into my diary', he said. 'No going back.'

I left a pregnant pause, in case he was joking. After the pregnancy, he was still grinning. Beneath the smile he was being deadly serious. The man had scheduled his happiness for 10 months hence. So, I did the obvious thing. I asked the only question I could. 'But it's February', I said. 'Why have you pencilled it in for November 1st?'

The guy looked at me and nodded knowingly. 'Oh, I've got a lot on', he explained. 'I'm managing a project at work. It's massive.

But it finishes at the end of October so I reckon November 1st is when I can start putting this wellbeing malarkey into practice.'

To this day, I'm still nonplussed by his answer. I mean, how far can you miss a point by? Just in case you were wondering, at no point have we suggested you schedule our rules into your diary. Or that you have a happy hour on a Thursday afternoon or invent 'Wellbeing Wednesday' when everyone in the office has to tell a joke.

We've been advocating that you etch the rules into your thinking and behaviours, so that you become a more positive person. It's not about *scheduling*, it's about *becoming*.

And we're suggesting you start NOW.

Why NOW?

Because NOW is all you ever have. Your entire life is lived in the present moment. All your history, all those memories, they can only ever be accessed from the present moment. As for your future? That doesn't exist. That wonderful holiday in three weeks' time, when you live it, will also be your present moment.

Our lingering delegate has kicked his happiness into the wet November grass. His message to himself is 'I've just got to get this project out of the way and then I'll be happy.'

> ## Timely advice?
>
> Don't just do something. *Sit there!*

The implications of the story above are massive.

You know that 4000-week average lifespan thing that we've been banging on about since page 1? Apologies, but we can now reveal that to be a BIG FAT LIE.

You haven't got 4000 weeks, you've only got NOW. Your life exists entirely in the present moment.

Buddhists have a phrase, tathātā, which is best translated as 'suchness' or the 'as-is-ness' of the moment. Enlightenment comes when you twig that the 'suchness of life' is, of course, no more than the *as-is-ness* of this moment.

This is deep, but worthwhile – opposition toward the moment is one of the main features of your human operating system. We rush through life, searching for the perfect moment. This lifelong pursuit means your mind is in a state of near permanent frustration. It doesn't want *this* moment, it wants a better one, in the future, so it's mad keen for you to get this moment out of the way. It makes you impatient with this 'now' without realizing that this particular now is all it ever has (that's because when it gets to the next now, that also becomes 'this now', hence your ego is in a never-ending chase for a better moment).

Back to tathātā, *this* moment – the only moment there ever is – is accepted and welcomed. It boils down to whether you want to make the present moment your friend or your foe. Remembering that the present moment is inseparable from life – 'now' is all you ever have – you're really deciding what kind of a relationship you want to have with life.

The entirety of our being is quietly revealed in the stillness of the moment. This points to something counter-intuitive: wisdom is not something we have to strive to acquire. Rather, it arises naturally as we slow down and notice what is already there.

Here's the depth. You might need to sit down for this. Befriending the present moment is befriending life itself.

Which means not only is NOW a *good* place to start, it's the *only* place to start, because it's all you've ever got.

Thank you for reading our rules.

Now go break some.

Index

ALSO BY ANDY COPE

The Art of Being Brilliant: Transform Your Life by Doing What Works For You

Andy Cope & Andy Whittaker

9780857083715

Shine: Rediscovering Your Energy, Happiness and Purpose

Andy Cope and Gavin Oattes

9780857087652

Be Brilliant Every Day

Andy Cope & Andy Whittaker

9780857085009

Zest: How to Squeeze the Max out of Life

Andy Cope, Gavin Oattes and Will Hussey

9780857088000

The Little Book of Being Brilliant

Andy Cope

9780857087973

·············· FOR KIDS AND TEENAGERS ··············

Diary of a Brilliant Kid: Top Secret Guide to Awesomeness

Andy Cope, Gavin Oattes and Will Hussey

9780857087867

The Art of Being a Brilliant Teenager

Andy Cope, Andy Whittaker, Darrell Woodman and Amy Bradley

9780857085788

Coming October 2020

A Girl's Guide to Being Fearless

Suzie Lavington and Andy Cope

9780857088574

CAPSTONE
A Wiley Brand